PARTNERSHIPS FOR IMPROVING SCHOOLS

Recent Titles in
Contributions to the Study of Education

PARTNERSHIPS FOR IMPROVING SCHOOLS

Byrd L. Jones *and* Robert W. Maloy

CONTRIBUTIONS TO THE STUDY OF EDUCATION,
NUMBER 24

GREENWOOD PRESS

New York
Westport, Connecticut
London

Library of Congress Cataloging-in-Publication Data

Jones, Byrd L.
   Partnerships for improving schools.

   (Contributions to the study of education,
ISSN 0196–707X ; no. 24)
   Bibliography: p.
   Includes index.
   1. School improvement programs—United States.
2. Community and school—United States.   3. Educational
innovations—United States.   I. Maloy, Robert W.
II. Title.   III. Series.
LB2822.82.J66   1988   371.1′04   87–23774
ISBN 0–313–25594–6 (lib. bdg. : alk. paper)

British Library Cataloguing in Publication Data is available.

Library of Congress Catalog Card Number: 87–23774
ISBN: 0–313–25594–6
ISSN: 0196–707X

First published in 1988

Greenwood Press, Inc.
88 Post Road West, Westport, Connecticut 06881

Printed in the United States of America

The paper used in this book complies with the
Permanent Paper Standard issued by the National
Information Standards Organization (Z39.48–1984).

10 9 8 7 6 5 4 3 2 1

Copyright Acknowledgments

Harvard University Press has graciously granted permission to reproduce Figure 3.1 from Robert Kegan, *The Evolving Self* (Cambridge: Harvard University Press, 1982). In addition, we have drawn from material earlier published in the following journals:

Maloy, R. W. (1985). The multiple realities of school-university collaboration. *The Educational Forum*, *49* (3), 341–50.

Jones, B. L., and Maloy, R. W. (1986). Collaboration and ill-structured problems of school improvement. *Planning & Changing*, *17* (1), 3–8.

Maloy, R. W., and Jones, B. L. (1987). Teachers, partnerships, and school improvement. *Journal of Research and Development in Education*, *20* (2), 19–24.

Contents

Figures

Acknowledgments

We deeply appreciate our good fortune in working with hundreds of partners for improving schools in Boston, Falmouth, Greenfield, Lawrence, Springfield, and Worcester, Massachusetts, as well as Roosevelt, New York, and Washington, D.C. We have learned much about the potentials of partnerships from positive and forceful administrative leaders, notably Ulysses Byas, Peter Clark, Carol A. Emery, Mario D. Fantini, Gordon Hargrove, Mary B. Koch, Cynthia McMullen, Robert Peterkin, John Simoncini, Eugene Thayer, and Miriam Williford. Many colleagues have demonstrated that reaching out to schools and communities enriches university life, including Lynn Cadwallader, Jimm DeShields, John E. Heffley, Barbara Love, A. Peter Mattaliano, Frank Rife, Harvey B. Scribner, and Earl Seidman.

We especially value the collaborative leadership, ongoing discussions about organizational change, and feedback on the manuscript offered by Richard J. Clark, Atron A. Gentry, and Susan D. Savitt. We have benefited greatly from careful reading and constructive comments on drafts of this book given by Sharon A. Edwards, Dana Fischetti, John Fischetti, Jeannie M. Jones, Joan Merrill, Carolyn C. Peelle, Mary Jo Reid, Mary Diotalevi Ryzcek, and Mary McCarthy Waight. We are grateful to Sheryl A. Jablonski and Joan M. Zabawa for their organizational skills and secretarial support; also we thank Jeffrey Eiseman for preparing the figures in Chapters 3 and 6.

Introduction

Over the past fifteen years, we have worked with a variety of school partnerships and have seen interorganizational arrangements promote both formal and informal learning for thousands of teachers in dozens of settings. When sustained over time through agreements and mutually beneficial projects, cooperative activities between teachers and members of outside organizations have tremendous potential for educational reform. We have learned that as educators arrive at new understandings about themselves, their colleagues, and their relationships to larger communities, they affect the learning climate for their students and the way other organizations interact with schools.

Building interorganizational linkages between schools and other organizations requires many levels of support, trust, volunteered efforts, and complex understandings of social realities. To date, most collaborative endeavors have emphasized one-way exchanges of people or resources that presume school deficiencies. Schools and parent/community groups, businesses, human service agencies, and institutions of higher education have separate interests, institutional dilemmas, and distinct ethos. Their interactions develop idiosyncratically, yet partnerships share common processes based on the culture of schools and the particular strategies and structures of other organizations.

Current enthusiasm for partnerships offers a window of opportunity for establishing communication around useful activities, and we have emphasized ways to support those positive forces. School improvements depend on a realistic and shared sense of educational purposes by teachers, school administrators, members of outside organizations, policymakers, and voters. Ideally, school people gain a sense of empowerment from mutually beneficial activities with outside groups that suggest alternative ways to learn and to teach. We hope this book will extend visions of fairer and more effective schools leading to a better future.

Drawing on documented accounts and our experiences, successive chapters present definitions of interactive partnerships; barriers to school improvement and the culture of schools; concepts for understanding interorganizational developments; modal developmental stages of a partnership; interests and purposes of outside organizations; cooperation and conflict within collaborative endeavors; teacher development and empowerment through interactions with others; interorganizational strategies and structures; leadership styles and assessments for collaborations; and school improvements and future societies.

In Part One, "A School Improvement Perspective," we argue that partnerships between schools and other organizations have empowered teachers and improved schools. Because partnerships involve both individual and organizational behaviors, any collaboration must affect the professional lives of teachers and the institutional cultures of schools. From the work of educators, phenomenological social scientists, and organizational theorists, we have derived three concepts—multiple realities, ill-structured problems, and reflexive thinking—that explicate the complex dynamics of interorganizational arrangements.

In Part Two, "Studies of Partnerships," we present a detailed study of a school-university project and scenarios of school interactions with parent/community groups, businesses, and human service agencies. Case studies and cross-case analyses of seven projects illustrate issues inherent in building organizational relationships based on the mutual interests and competing purposes of potential partners. Evidence from specific settings and theoretical concepts are juxtaposed to show how cooperation or competition may emerge within school improvement activities.

In Part Three, "Evolving Understandings," we analyze common dynamics and processes found in partnerships from the distinct standpoints of teachers, organizations, leaders, and the larger society. Improvements in schools emerge as teachers explore their professional roles and dilemmas with others, as organizations reframe complex or ill-structured problems, and as leaders support alternatives that encourage experimentation. Over time, interactive processes between schools and outside organizations foster evolving understandings of education and better futures.

In the text, where sources are not indicated, the information comes from project files in the School of Education at the University of Massachusetts or in the authors' possession. All italics within quotations were in the original. We have corrected obvious typographical errors within quotations and followed current American Psychological Association guidelines in capitalizing Black and White throughout.

PART ONE

A SCHOOL IMPROVEMENT PERSPECTIVE

1

The Promise of
School Partnerships

Not long ago, several teachers in a rural Massachusetts elementary school and a university professor unlocked a closet containing scientific equipment. The materials had been stored two decades earlier when the building had served as a high school. While looking through the boxes, the teachers discussed ideas for hands-on science lessons using the electrical devices. Their exploration had been occasioned through a partnership involving a utility firm, a university, and several school systems. Working with colleagues and outside partners, the teachers created new curriculum and new relationships.

Northeast Utilities had initiated cooperative activities in order to promote positive attitudes toward energy conservation among teachers. The firm then asked the University of Massachusetts at Amherst to coordinate workshops and to offer academic credits. School administrators supported the project as a way to update the curriculum. Participating teachers learned more than scientific facts and gained more than graduate credits (H. Doyle, personal communication, April 18, 1985). One teacher overcame her childhood fears about "things that were electrical or mechanical." She noted that "kids are quick to pick up on a teacher's uneasiness, so I kept my science lessons confined to what I knew well."

Reflecting on their experiences some months later, the teachers agreed that opening the storage room had initiated fresh possibilities for teaching and learning. "My science anxiety has been dispelled," a teacher enthused. "I am using the microscope and the motors and plan to make some changes in my other lessons as well." Further, students designed their own experiments. The partnership also provoked discussions among adults. "This has been a wonderful experience for us," explained another teacher. "There has been a real sense of sharing between people from industry, the University, other teachers, and even the children. I am co-teaching a science lesson once a week."

This vignette concerning activities and attitudes in an elementary school introduces some key themes about partnerships. Outsiders working with teachers can stimulate group projects and communications that lead to new instructional and organizational patterns. Discovering ways to modify their behaviors, teachers use modest resources to improve their curriculum and invent alternative approaches. As two researchers concluded, "1) schools, if they are to improve or be improved, must somehow be connected to new knowledge from the outside and 2) conditions within the schools have to be such that staff members can share this new knowledge among themselves" (Tye and Tye, 1984, p. 319).

Effective partnerships generate activities and discussions that reveal personal doubts or professional dilemmas and help unblock stalemated group processes or stable organizational structures. Voluntary cooperation around shared activities between schools and parent/community groups, businesses, human service agencies, or universities promotes growth for individuals and organizations that seldom occurs in isolated or static settings. Moreover, such collaborative efforts need not require large-scale or costly additions to staff, instructional materials, and other resources.

PARTNERSHIPS AS SCHOOL REFORM

In response to local initiatives as well as publicity about collaborative school reforms, public schools have entered into a multitude of formal agreements with outside organizations. During 1983–1984, more than 15,000 schools were engaged in voluntary partnerships with some 46,000 outside sponsors (United States Department of Education, 1984). These arrangements have provided schools with tutors, other volunteers, materials for resource centers, sites for special programs, and added support for extracurricular and staff development activities. In addition, most districts have sponsored parent-teacher associations, recreational leagues, placements for student teachers, and work-training programs.

Research studies and national reports have advocated closer ties between schools and other organizations (Boyer, 1983; Cetron, 1985; Comer, 1980; Eurich, 1985; Goodlad, 1984; Lombana, 1983; Maeroff, 1983; Madaus, Airasian, and Kellaghan, 1980; National Commission on Excellence in Education, 1983; Task Force on Education for Economic Growth, 1983; National Science Board Commission on Precollege Education in Mathematics, Science and Technology, 1983; College Board, 1984). According to these authors, parent groups (especially those representing low-income or minority neighborhoods), potential employers, human service agencies, and institutions of higher education should contribute fresh perspectives and resources to teachers in schools.

A reform's popularity cannot assure its success. Since World War II, Americans have focused on various strategies for school improvement including "new math," flexible scheduling, desegregation, educational television, management by objectives, open classrooms, competency-based curricula, microcomputers, master teacher or merit pay plans, teacher preparation programs, and "mainstreaming" special needs students. Federal, state and local governments have allocated billions of dollars to modify teacher training, instructional practices, educational technologies, administrative structures, texts, and curricula. The social and economic crises of the past four decades have lent urgency to these reforms: "Sputnik in 1957; civil rights in the 1960s; the Vietnam War in the 1970s; and the recession of the early 1980s, as our manufacturing industries lost their competitive advantage over foreign competitors" (Kirst, 1984, p. 8).

Most reform efforts have fallen short of their sponsors' expectations because they have affected only part of complex educational systems. According to Passow (1986), school improvement "must involve changes in the knowledge, skills, attitudes, understandings, and values of staff; in the organizational relationships of the school; in the climate and environment of the school; and in the transactions between teachers and learners" (p. 216). Can partnerships between schools and outside organizations support activities among diverse individuals that allow time to learn new perspectives and approaches, to share activities and understandings, and to reconsider organizational strategies and structures? Our answer is affirmative—if collaboration empowers teachers as professionals to interact with outsiders to renew a sense of educational purposes.

COLLABORATIVE INTERCHANGES

To date, most educators have sought outside partners who would respond to manifest needs with personnel or material resources. Such "you have/we need" interchanges brought publicity without long-term or open-ended commitments. Because schools lack resources, teachers and administrators have generally welcomed contributions, such as the following selections from a list of over fifty ideas for linkages with businesses:

5) Companies donate computers to schools and train school staff. . . .

10) Companies provide puppet shows and participate in assembly programs stressing good health, safety, and character building. . . .

15) Company donates a popcorn machine to the student body. . . .

20) Companies sponsor trips to state capitol for leadership class. . . .

25) Volunteers assist with student participation in Special Olympics. . . .

30) Companies provide eyeglasses and doctor's care to needy students. . . .

35) School graduation is held on company facilities. (Reed, 1986, p. 50)

When a "you have/we need" approach dominates partnerships, then formal agreements define the parameters of cooperation. The above list, for instance, limited expectations to ways that businesses might help schools. Few changes in personal perspectives or organizational behaviors emerge from well-defined agreements, such as when parents serve as advisory board members, human service agency personnel help evaluate children with special needs, or universities offer tuition waivers to teachers who supervise interns. Those interchanges seldom evolve over time, engage only a few individuals, respond mainly to surface problems, and rarely touch the underlying ethos of participating organizations.

Most relationships involving schools and outside organizations can be located along a continuum from separation through communication and cooperation to collaboration (Wise, 1981). Traditionally, educators have communicated with parents, business leaders, human service staffs, and higher education faculty about their needs while maintaining separate spheres of activity. Closer ties have occurred when outsiders provided resources to assist schools in specific areas. Wise (1981) urged businesses to ask how schools can be more responsive to the needs of employers and to examine joint "educational functions of both schools and employers" (p. 79).

Just as a person's close friendships grow from many polite interchanges with others, interactive partnerships capable of altering organizational perspectives and structures may evolve from a wide array of "you have/we need" arrangements. Those developments require communicating, building trust, sharing personal assessments of strengths and weaknesses, verifying those judgments through common endeavors, and gaining new perspectives. Partnerships also involve endorsements from leaders, substructures for governance, formal processes for assessment and renegotiation, and understandings about overlapping interests and distinct institutional purposes.

MUTUAL INTERESTS AND COMPETING PURPOSES

Individuals and organizations share a self-interest in better education—whatever their personal or institutional purposes. Schooling is widely perceived by the public as intimately connected with most young Americans' preparation for adult responsibilities. The interests of parent/

community groups, businesses, human service agencies, and institutions of higher education overlap with schools. Outside groups want educational success, but they also want schools to emphasize certain priorities. Thus, school partnerships may exacerbate persistent tensions and political pressures around the purposes of schooling.

Teachers and their partners offer varied, "personal" descriptions of what are ostensibly the same context. For instance, parents have identified discipline as their key concern, business leaders have asked for basic skills training, human service agencies have contended that schools ignore many family and personal problems, and universities have complained about poor writing skills among incoming students. Those multiple perspectives have occasioned not only differing opinions about specific events, but also serious disagreements about the overall purposes and priorities of partnerships.

Parents and other adults in households with children are directly concerned about the daily experiences and learning achievements of their youngsters. Some parents press to transfer their child to a "better" teacher without expressing concern for others who may be relegated to a "worse" teacher. Families and local community institutions depend on schools to foster in students a reasonable socialization, respect for property, and readiness for adult responsibilities as citizens and workers. With property taxes typically covering 40 to 50 percent of public school costs, local taxpayers dislike expensive programs; but they support funds for substantive and useful training.

Businesses have both a general interest in competent citizens as consumers and a particular interest in a well-trained labor supply. Most workers and firms benefit from basic skills in spelling, computing, writing, adhering to instructions and time schedules, and completing assignments without careless errors. Neatness does matter in the real world. Often firms seek to shift some of their training costs, such as for typing from dictation or word processing, back to schools and the taxpayers. Increasingly, employers seek self-starters who can complete responsibilities without directives and supervision. Somehow, schools are expected to train individuals to take orders, to give orders, or to work independently—depending on the circumstances.

Many human service agencies supplement school responses to student and family needs. Poverty and mental or physical health problems can interfere with student learning. Abused children need public support in addition to what schools can provide. Families, schools, and communities all suffer from individuals who are involved with substance abuse or petty crimes. Mandates for "mainstreaming" children with special needs or desegregating schools often involve outside professionals or mediation services. Furthermore, communities support a rich array of nonformal educational organizations—Girl Scouts, Boys' Clubs,

4–H, religious training groups, recreational leagues, and neighborhood centers—with which schools may establish mutually beneficial ventures.

Institutions of higher education draw students from secondary schools and hence will benefit from educational reforms. The readiness of high school graduates determines the level of general education requirements, core courses, and ultimately the quality of higher education. Many college graduates explore teaching as a career, and their successes and failures reflect on higher education and specific teacher preparation programs. In a world of rapid scientific and technological discovery, teachers must continually translate new knowledge and paradigms into an articulated curriculum from kindergarten through the doctoral level.

There are other potential connections between outside groups and schools—linkages to state education centers or regional research organizations, pairings of schools (elementary and secondary or public and private), or "adoptions" by a professional athletic team, musical group or community club. A firm may be linked to schools through community volunteers or the election of an employee to the district school committee. Many local service organizations have provided scholarships, athletic equipment or band uniforms. Ordinarily such informal, temporary arrangements depend on civic-minded individuals with community spirit.

Formal collaborations between schools and outside organizations include diverse perspectives and unstated agendas. Despite their common interest in good schools, organizations develop missions and objectives around their own purposes. The possibilities of shifting costs and responsibilities to the other partner fosters mistrust. Thus, when outside partners urge stricter discipline for children, vocational training for potential employees, responsiveness to special needs children, or rapid dissemination of technological breakthroughs, they raise issues of competing values and means.

DYNAMICS OF COLLABORATION

In principle, voluntary partnerships enable organizations to share tasks, maximize resource utilization, and serve both mutually shared and unique self-interests. Thus, teachers extend their definitions of education beyond their own classrooms. Recent partnerships in Little Rock (Arkansas), Atlanta (Georgia), Richmond (Virginia), and Boston (Massachusetts) illustrate how working together can both meet immediate needs and enlarge a school's sense of purpose.

In Little Rock, officials from the public school system, the University of Arkansas, and a local human service agency created an "extended day school" (Caldwell, 1986). Locating early childhood and elementary programs in the same building naturally linked infancy, preschool and primary education. Children received developmentally continuous curriculum, parents gained greater access to child care, and the university acquired a field site for the preservice and inservice preparation of teachers.

An "adopt-a-school" program in Atlanta has brought schools together with community businesses, service organizations, governmental agencies, and churches (Fraser, 1985). Part of the Atlanta Partnership for Business and Education, the program provided field trips, music programs, speakers, internships, new and used books, awards, and other assistance to elementary and secondary school students. By getting outside their schools, students could learn from the richly varied resources of the Atlanta community.

In Virginia, 40 businesses and community agencies in the Richmond Private Industry Council founded a "New Horizons" program for low-income, non–college bound students in the eleventh and twelfth grades. The program introduced students to available career opportunities through formal courses that emphasized basic job survival skills. This on-site training utilized current technologies and equipment. Thus, "schools benefit by having a curriculum which motivates students to do well" while "business benefits from improved access to entry level employees who are much better prepared than has been generally true" (McNett, 1982, p. 88).

For over a decade, 24 colleges and universities in Boston have been paired with selected public schools. Established by a federal court's school desegregation order in 1975, these pairings enabled institutions of higher education to help with "research, curriculum and staff development, data management, tutoring and other supplemental services to students" (Cohen, 1985, p. 23). Judge Arthur Garrity and others believed that breaking down barriers of racial isolation required the combined support of Boston's key educational and business institutions.

Given the presence of personal mistrust and institutional differences, partnerships—that are widely advocated and seemingly beneficial to all partners—often require an external mandate to get started. In Little Rock, project planners faced problems in overcoming longstanding antipathies between child care providers and elementary teachers. The Atlanta system aggressively marketed "adoptions." In Boston, a desegregation order mandated a link between schools and outside organizations. Sustaining such partnerships has required the efforts of a few individuals whose personal charisma and dedication have encouraged others to participate.

Most partnerships have engendered frustration, breakdowns in communication, and conflict among participants (Sarason, 1982; Trubowitz et al., 1984), and even relatively successful ones have experienced difficulties. Typically, an initial period of excitement with visions of potential benefits gives way to contradictory versions of reality, overt and covert conflicts, and diminished commitments to the relationship. Seymour Sarason (1984) analyzed why so few partnerships succeed. People in schools "look at 'outsiders' with suspicion" and interorganizational linkages occasion "two cultures misunderstanding and clashing with each other" (p. 19). Thus, partners experience "complexity, unpredictability and uncontrollability of the total situation" (p. 24).

A better understanding of the complex dynamics of partnerships increases the likelihood that people from schools and other organizations will sustain and nurture collaborations long enough to generate positive outcomes. The creation of a new setting requires individuals both to gain perspectives on their roles as members of an organization and to consider alternative group strategies and structures. Those processes require time for productive interactions and reflection.

INTERACTIVE PARTNERSHIPS

Asked to design a school improvement project, a group of teachers in a course offered through a partnership agreed to reinvigorate "Know Your School Night." They talked with the principal and colleagues. They asked language teachers to translate a letter for parents into Greek and Spanish. They prepared an informational display about their collaborative project and its Community Council, and they designed an assessment instrument to obtain feedback from parents. Attendance increased remarkably, and they documented both the group process and its outcomes. Beyond those immediate benefits, they rediscovered an ability to work with colleagues.

Other participants in the course implemented a variety of projects. One working group prepared an extensive survey of students' attitudes toward life in the school, their teachers and their peers. Another group assembled informational brochures about school policies and the community in order to help over 50 students who had enrolled after the September orientation period. Some teachers included multicultural elements in their curriculum while others helped their students cope with mainstreaming. Through progress reports, formal presentations, and informal discussions around refreshments during class breaks, teachers shared their hopes and problems.

Current research on partnerships and change has depicted the complexity of cooperative problem-solving relationships in organizational cultures. As Sarason (1982) observed, "you can have the most creative, compellingly valid, educationally productive idea in the world, but whether it can become embedded and sustained in a socially complex setting will be primarily a function of how you conceptualize the implementation-change process" (p. 78). Studies of effective schools have emphasized interactive processes "based on joint problem-solving and a set of commonly held beliefs, norms, and practices" (Olson, 1986, p. 12).

We envision partnerships between schools and other organizations as a series of shared incentives and interactive endeavors that involve more than delivering a service and then assessing its success or failure. Partners have much to learn from interactive exchanges. These interorganizational linkages create organizational substructures that exist outside the direct control of the participating institutions. Cooperation is generated by the movement of ideas, resources and people back and forth between organizations. Goals and objectives are not specifically defined in advance, but emerge and shift as the partners negotiate the terms of their mutual efforts. As an approach to educational reform, such partnerships are practical, cost-effective and highly promising.

Our case for an interactive approach to educational collaboration rests on three major propositions. First, when teachers associate with colleagues and people from other organizations to exchange benefits, partnerships generate mutual learning processes. That empowerment counteracts the frustration, isolation, and organizational stasis experienced by many educators. When sustained over time, communication about personal and organizational constraints is enriched. Second, as people from different organizations (or different parts of the same organization) interact, participants play new roles and develop new relationships. Experiencing new activities in different settings fosters both personal and organizational growth and development (Bronfenbrenner, 1979; Kegan, 1982). Third, after learning new roles and experiencing other organizational cultures, partners infuse daily activities with alternative understandings about teaching and education.

Collaborative processes are thus more significant than specific activities and immediately discernible outcomes. The following checklist suggests some of the common features of interactive partnerships between schools and other organizations:

1. They involve new resources from parent and community groups, businesses, human service agencies, and institutions of higher education.
2. They promote a sharing of information, resources, time, and talent that helps people think about better schools.
3. They seek greater utilization of community resources rather than raising revenues for more of the same things.
4. They reduce the isolation of students, teachers and schools through association with other powerful groups.
5. They encourage decision making and problem solving on a local level by those most affected by the outcomes.
6. They are voluntary, cooperative and flexible.

STUDIES OF COLLABORATIVE PROJECTS

We have learned about the dynamics of collaborative developments and the advantages of interactive processes through our involvements with seven significant projects associated with the School of Education at the University of Massachusetts at Amherst. These partnerships involved many of the same individuals, a common institutional framework, and school systems facing similar problems and resources. Hence, we have focused on outcomes associated with differences among activities, processes and interactive scenarios. We have compared our evolving insights with the understandings of many other individuals in these as well as dozens of other collaborative projects in other parts of the country.

Education for Community Service Program (ECS), 1973–1981. A cooperative project between the University and the Falmouth (Massachusetts) Public Schools, ECS linked teachers, university faculty, and community human service workers in a master's degree program designed to expand the use of community resources in the schools and extend instructional competencies to human service agencies. When key staff and supporters moved on and many teachers had benefited, the project was phased out by mutual agreement.

Boston Secondary Schools Project (BSSP), 1974– . A school improvement/staff development partnership between the University and secondary schools in the Boston metropolitan area, the project began at English High School in 1974. Subsequently, BSSP expanded to include twenty school-based improvement teams, and more than 120 teachers and administrators participated in 1985. In 1979, the project received a Distinguished Achievement Award from the American Association of Colleges for Teacher Education. More than 70 students have earned graduate degrees.

Greenfield Secondary Schools Project, 1978–1981. A collaboration among the Greenfield (Massachusetts) Public Schools, local parents and community members, the State Department of Education, and the University, the project examined parent, teacher, and student attitudes toward schools; developed grant-funded programs; and tried to integrate special education students into the regular education system. Following initial difficulties, the project provided minigrants to teachers and sponsored a dropout prevention/playground development effort with community support.

Worcester Teacher Corps Project, 1979–1982. A staff development program sponsored by Teacher Corps that involved the Worcester (Massachusetts) Public Schools, a local Community Council composed of parents and community residents and the University, the project improved school learning climates, enhanced teacher effectiveness and revitalized ties between schools and their communities in four Worcester schools serving low-income neighborhoods. The project ended when federal funds were eliminated.

Lawrence Teacher Academy, 1981–1982. A cooperative effort of the Lawrence (Massachusetts) Public Schools and the University, the Teacher Academy addressed the professional and personal development needs of teachers in an urban school system experiencing rapid shifts in the racial-ethnic character of its student population. University faculty offered workshops, graduate classes, and consultations for three academic semesters; but long-term agreements for staff development did not materialize.

Roosevelt/UMass Staff Development Project, 1982– . A staff development/school improvement partnership between the University and the Roosevelt (New York) Public Schools, located on Long Island, the project supports cooperative activities to promote overall district improvement. In 1985, this project received an Exemplary Staff Development Model Award from the American Association of School Administrators.

Math English Science Technology Education Project (MESTEP), 1982– . A fifth-year teacher certification partnership involving the University of Massachusetts, Digital Equipment Corporation, other high technology businesses, and school systems located along Massachusetts' high technology corridor, the project uses public and private sector cooperation to recruit and prepare secondary-level mathematics and science teachers. Over a fifteen-month cycle, 24 students earn an M.Ed. degree and certification while interning in both firms and classrooms. MESTEP received the 1986 Distinguished Achievement Award from the American Association of Colleges for Teacher Education for "innovation in the preparation of science and mathematics teachers."

Every partnership is embedded in time and place with its own dynamics, characteristics, personalities, and scenarios for change. A boundless number of variables may affect a change process—including type of school, kind of community, racial and ethnic patterns, leadership styles, income levels, and teacher characteristics. Furthermore, many important results are the indirect or unintended consequences of other planned options. Changes in schools that occur during partnerships are always connected to a larger context of people, organizations and communities.

The partnerships we studied most closely were affected by (1) the involvement of a university dedicated to public service, (2) staff development for an experienced instructional force, and (3) multiple organizational partners. Since 1969, the School of Education at the University of Massachusetts at Amherst has been publicly committed to developing new educational models that emphasize innovation, outreach, diversity, equity and school reform. These projects involved issues of race and class, of special needs and bilingual education, and of multicultural curriculum and multiracial staffs.

These projects also reflect external and programmatic realities that dominated American education during the 1970s and 1980s. Educational systems in the Northeast experienced declining enrollments, rising costs and inflationary pressures, diminished federal support, few new teachers (except for special education and bilingual programs), and resistance among taxpayers to increased spending for public education. That context shaped an emphasis on educational change projects that concentrated on staff development and better uses of existing resources by schools and communities (Dillon-Peterson, 1981). Although rising school enrollments in some areas will bring demands for new teachers, advocates and supporters of partnerships will face a similar context over the next five to ten years.

A NOTE ON METHODOLOGY

Case studies are appropriate for empirical investigations of "a contemporary phenomenon within its real-life context; when the boundaries between phenomenon and context are not clearly evident; and in which multiple sources of evidence are used" (Yin, 1984, p. 23). For over a decade, we have been involved as participants and observers in a wide variety of school improvement projects. We have asked how and why specific partnerships have developed and evolved—how they have overcome barriers to school improvement (Chapter 2) and established inter-organizational cooperation. Drawing on analytical concepts from the social sciences, we have asked why multiple realities, ill-structured problems, and reflexive thinking characterize viable partnerships (Chapter 3).

We have sought to understand organizational ethos and change processes from a set of values associated with ethnographic approaches: "phenomenology, holism, nonjudgmental orientation, and contextualism" (Fetterman, 1984, p. 23). This approach involves almost unimaginable quantities and varieties of relevant information. Complex descriptions interweave individual and/or organizational perspectives with broad economic, political and social factors. Our own observations and responses as well as those of others have been examined within a contextual framework. We have also compared our observations and responses with those made by others and with historical and sociological evidence of partnership developments.

After collecting substantial information on many partnerships, we constructed a formal protocol for case studies to assure the completeness of our data base. We used needs assessments, project documents, reports and evaluations, seminar papers and doctoral dissertations, directed and nondirected interviews, and our own participation and observations to assemble reasonably comprehensive files for each project. For each stage of partnerships—from "prehistory" to formal agreements, implementation of activities, and assessment and evolving understandings—we learned about specific factors, processes and characteristics.

In the case of prehistory, we examined early linkages between organizational partners, surrounding assumptions about collaboration, core interests and separate missions, as well as political and educational contexts. In considering formal agreements, we sought information about key participants including initiators, implementers, supporters, detractors and bystanders; individual and institutional costs and benefits; trust-building and key negotiations; and contracts and other memorandums of understanding. Implementation of activities covered staffing and participants, planned activities, communications and public relations, substructures for delivery of services, and substructures for governance. To determine effectiveness and evolving understandings, we collected data on project assessments by participants and evaluators, midcourse corrections, and unanticipated outcomes and new directions.

We did not draft reports for each partnership. Instead, we have followed Yin (1984) in using a "cross-case analysis" that is both "explanatory" and "exploratory" (p. 129). In Chapter 4, we present one project in a chronological and detailed format in order to illustrate a typical developmental pattern. Chapters 5 through 9 offer cross-case generalizations drawn from the details of specific projects and illustrated by "abbreviated vignettes" (p. 129). Our presentations follow a "theory-building logic" (p. 133) from multiple realities of phenomenology to ill-structured problems, while shifting emphasis from teachers' roles to school organizations.

We recognize a bias in our approach, although it has some justification. Believing that schools can offer a better education for students and that ongoing changes are essential to create better future societies, we discuss in depth those aspects of partnerships that have worked well. By describing the difficulties of interorganizational cooperation and a conservative culture pervading schools, we acknowledge that there are ample reasons for partnerships to fall short of their potential. We have not, however, described those shortcomings either systematically or in detail.

Although we recognize that few partnerships have flourished without dedicated leaders, we have consciously downplayed charismatic leadership. Sarason (1982) has noted a tendency to attribute outcomes to personal characteristics, especially of leaders, without comprehending "that individuals operate in various social settings that have a structure not comprehensible by our existing theories of individual personality"

(p. 26). Leaders influence outcomes through interactions with groups and project-specific scenarios. Hence, we focus on interactive processes and discuss leadership in terms of typical issues experienced during interoganizational activities (Chapter 9).

Both participants in school change and outside observers frequently exaggerate the expected outcomes for school improvement. Although every reformer would like gains in student esteem and satisfaction with school, as well as academic achievement, few interventions are large enough relative to the forces affecting schools to show statistically significant gains over five to ten years. Specific projects with narrow goals such as reducing tardiness or raising scores on a fifth-grade writing test often produce solid gains but typically ignore other areas where new problems may arise.

We believe significant improvement involves a change in school cultures. According to Purkey and Smith (1983), this approach

assumes that changing schools requires changing people's behaviors and attitudes, as well as school organization and norms. It assumes that consensus among the staff of a school is more powerful than overt control, without ignoring the need for leadership. Building staff agreement on specified norms and goals becomes the focus of any school improvement strategy. (pp. 441–42)

The problem of exaggerated hopes for school improvement and indirect relationships between inputs and effects on students are peculiarly acute for school improvement projects. First, as low-cost, voluntaristic projects, partnerships set vague or broad goals to allow for later developments. Second, the disproportion between a $15,000 budget for the Roosevelt Staff Development Project and the district's $20 million budget or funding of approximately $60,000 for BSSP and the Boston Public Schools' $200 million annual budget suggests the difficulty of discerning measurable changes in student achievements based on collaborative activities. On the other hand, collaborative activities with their mixture of insider-outsider perspectives and flexible mandates for improvements are almost ideally suited to open possibilities for positive interactions that affect school cultures.

We considered five key components for case studies as identified by Yin (1984): (1) a study's questions, (2) its underlying propositions, (3) its units of analysis, (4) logic connecting evidence to propositions, and (5) criteria for interpreting findings (p. 29). Initially we asked what happens to collaborative projects. A series of subsidiary issues arose—most partnerships prove troublesome, differences in perspectives develop among partners, goals and objectives often lack clarity, team-building is difficult, and discouragement and frustration override early hopes for cooperative success. Over time, many partnerships settle into routine exchanges of services involving a handful of members of each organization. We concluded that describing and analyzing why partnerships fail was neither difficult nor particularly useful.

In this sense, partnerships resemble other highly touted innovations for schools that have floundered. But the literature on collaboration—in combination with studies of effective schools—has suggested how changes have taken hold in those schools where leadership and support have led to adoption and adaptation of a curriculum that emphasizes learning, regular monitoring, an orderly environment, and high expectations for students and staff. This literature suggested that shared processes and procedures might characterize viable partnerships. Thus, we asked how successful collaborations support activities among diverse individuals that allow time to learn new perspectives and approaches, to reconsider purposes of education, and to reflect on shared understandings and activities.

We have learned much from the work of Ronald Edmonds, Carol Gilligan, Robert Kegan, Ann Lieberman and Lynne Miller, Michael Lipsky, Ian Mitroff, Seymour Sarason, Alfred Schutz, and Karl Weick. Their insights were confirmed and enriched by the work of literally hundreds of teachers and students who have contributed their efforts and thoughts to collaborative endeavors. Researchers, teachers and students illustrate that the key to school improvement rests in establishing and maintaining a spirit of purposeful change based on the strengths and realities present in public schools today.

Accordingly, we agreed on the following propositions. Public schools in the United States resemble closed systems or self-perpetuating cultures that will be less and less functional for future societies. School improvement must involve sustained efforts by educators to involve new resources and to introduce different behaviors into school settings. Because schools behave like loosely coupled systems—or organizations already overloaded by demands—outside mandates or additional dollars budgeted for more of the same activities seldom achieve their intended effects. Few collaborations flourish without an understanding of school cultures, the dilemmas of service faced by teachers, phenomenological visions of all participants, and relevant pressures on all partners. Partnerships with parent/community groups, businesses, human service agencies, or institutions of higher education offer new resources and perspectives over a period of time that can foster school improvement.

We have examined partnerships as developmental projects with typical stages over a life cycle. We considered specific processes and activities that resolved problems. We assumed that activities in a school affect the attitudes of those involved in ways that influence their educational strategies and suggest new organizational structures. After drafting our descriptions of school change, we shared these patterns with teachers who experienced a "shock of recognition." We believe they saw logical connections between our analytic propositions and their firsthand knowledge of collaborative developments. Changes in teacher outlooks, school organizational patterns, and building climate or environment provide a framework for addressing deeper issues of curriculum and instruction.

Ultimately, we assert that if schools and outside organizations work together over time, they will gain fresh perspectives, redefine the nature of their partnership, and reflect on the purposes of educational reforms. Accordingly, we define collaborative "success" or "effectiveness" as changing teacher attitudes and/or school behaviors through group processes that share power and enhance the equity of outcomes. Successful partnerships will generate new understandings, improve the educational quality of schools, and negotiate means and goals toward a future society.

2
Teachers, School Climate, and Professional Development

Approximately 40 million students attend more than 80 thousand schools, employing 2 million teachers at a cost exceeding $125 billion annually—about 5 percent of personal income in the United States. For most parents, education is an investment in their children's future prospects; yet teachers and districts generally appear unresponsive to requests by students or parents for better schools. Teachers can make only limited adjustments for one student's interests and concerns when they have another two dozen in their classrooms. Aiming to maintain an orderly environment for several hundred energetic children and a reasonably structured curriculum across age levels, school staffs create a bureaucratic and alienating climate.

Anyone observing schools during opening week in September discovers an incredible montage of hopes and fears, long-term plans and short-term coping tactics, formal learning objectives, and informal socialization. Most students arrive already acculturated to remembered school routines, but five-year olds and transfers share apprehensions as well as anticipations. Seniors look ahead to graduation and adult responsibilities. Families and students need support, guidance and role models that both conserve traditions and prepare for future economic and social roles. Today's schools are expected to convey public values and national purposes while preparing young adults for their places in a complex postindustrial society.

Teachers clarify their procedures and expectations for an orderly classroom, get to know 30 to 150 individuals by name and personality, and hope to enliven learning for all their students during the coming months. Some worry about taking an inservice course, teaching a different grade level or subject, or adjusting to personal concerns. Others are preoccupied by a second job or hobby. Some mark time till retirement. Principals and counselors respond to individual concerns, and they hope order will ensue when students become familiar with classes, teachers, buses, schedules, and school discipline codes.

Children from age five through eighteen attend school some six hours a day, 180 days a year in a national system of education. Ordinarily, they learn enough to get through the rest of their lives. Teachers help most of their students much of the time. Staff remain excited about human development and administrators adjust bureaucratic rules and academic schedules to fit individual needs. As complex social systems, however, schools seldom achieve equitable outcomes, especially for poor and minority students and those with special needs. Schools proclaim equal opportunity and meritocratic standards while perpetuating a society differentiated by race, class, gender, religion, ethnic origin, region, and accepted values. Schools are age-segregated, teacher-dominated, bureaucratically scheduled, and norm-referenced institutions—although learning is none of the above.

On the whole, schools replicate the social hierarchy that students bring with them; and they limp along with ineffectual leaders, muddled curricular goals, low expectations, and fuzzy standards. In most schools, teachers have grown accustomed to existing conditions, seldom share their clinical expertise about curriculum, and lack organizational skills to adopt and adapt innovations over a sustained period of time. In a sense, the characteristics of successful innovations (McLaughlin and Marsh, 1978; Berman and McLaughlin, 1978), of effective schools (Edmonds, 1982), and of successful improvement efforts (Lieberman and Miller, 1984; Lehming and Kane, 1981) have described a typical school from a reverse angle.

Partnerships will prove a weak remedy unless they reduce deep-seated obstacles to teacher development and school improvement. Outside collaborators and potential school partners must comprehend how professional experiences and institutional cultures shape the understandings, perspectives and expectations of insiders. As ordinarily experienced by their staffs, schools involve complex roles related to "learning alone in groups." Classroom management and bureaucratic record keeping conflict with individual human development. Social pressures for equitable outcomes continually challenge both students and teachers.

BARRIERS TO CHANGE

An experienced English teacher reflected on his increasingly "realistic" expectations. "You've got to take chances, or you never get anywhere," he insisted. "I gave those kids a hundred and five percent. But I can't do that all the time. One of my ideals used to be, and I think it's typical of beginning teachers, that I'm going to reach all these kids. It's bullshit. You can't do that." He questioned homogeneous tracking; "you can't even group two kids together. You've got a class with some kid that's a virtual parsnip, and in the same class you've got another kid who is a very sensitive, creative, seeking, striving kind of kid" (Raphael, 1985, p. 45).

In his classic study of *Life in Classrooms*, Philip W. Jackson (1968) uncovered a general sense of powerlessness: "The teacher's concern with the here-and-now and her emotional attachment to her world was often accompanied in her conversations by an accepting attitude toward educational conditions as they presently exist" (p. 148). Challenged by 200 to 300 interpersonal interchanges each hour of the day while managing 25 to 30 children and attempting to follow a standard curriculum, teachers have little time for planning or reflection. "Lacking a technical vocabulary, skimming the intellectual surface of the problems they encounter, fenced in, as it were, by the walls of their concrete experience, these teachers hardly look like the type of people who should be allowed to supervise the intellectual development of young children" (Jackson, 1968, p. 148). Yet good teachers must act personally in order to humanize the standards and customary practices imposed by schools as bureaucratic organizations.

Charles Silberman's *Crisis in the Classroom* (1970) found that despite uncounted reform attempts, "the schools themselves are largely unchanged" (p. 159). He observed activity without consciousness of larger purpose:

But if one looks at what actually goes on in the classroom—the kinds of texts students read and the kind of homework they are assigned, as well as the nature of classroom discussion and the kinds of tests teachers give—he will discover that the great bulk of students' time is still devoted to detail, most of it trivial, much of it factually incorrect, and almost all of it unrelated to any concept, structure, cognitive strategy, or indeed anything other than the lesson plan. It is rare to find anyone—teacher, principal, supervisor or superintendent—who has asked why he is teaching what he is teaching. (pp. 172–73)

Despite shifts in instructional techniques and new knowledge, school organizational structures have remained remarkably the same for decades.

In *The One Best System: A History of American Urban Education* (1974), David Tyack traced the historical development of city superintendents who promoted standardization of classrooms and curriculum with Carnegie units and certified teachers. By adopting features of a factory model that included interchangeable classroom instruction with supervision vested in a principal, administrators could impose their ideas for good instruction on teachers—many of whom had offered an inferior curriculum. In doing so, these reformers created a system in which only large, district-wide changes seemed possible. A new mathematics or reading curriculum apparently required sequenced texts and objectives for each grade level. Evaluation would remain tentative till kindergartners had graduated using the new materials.

Karl Weick (1979) has argued succinctly that organizations exist to sustain predictable behaviors. Second-grade teachers accept discipline codes for their building, cover learning objectives defined by state guidelines, and prepare their students for the third grade. Cooks and cafeteria aides or textbook representatives can count on regular schedules and common tastes. These embedded practices allow for an appearance of local control, although curriculum and scheduling are so common that most students can transfer to another school, even across state boundaries, at any time during the year without major disruption.

Yet Weick (1976, 1982) found educational systems "loosely coupled" so that neither innovations nor additional resources produced the expected outcomes. School administrators and reformers have responded by tightening controls and demanding accountability. On the other hand, a flexible system of diverse subparts and ill-structured problems may have given schools a useful stability enabling teachers to cope with rapid shifts in public demands and technological transformations. Had schools responded to each highly touted reform, they would have zigged and zagged, entailing staff retraining and new materials.

According to Sarason (1971, 1972, 1982), the culture of schools was complexly interrelated so that curricular changes were "washed out" by management regularities and deeper values imposed by a system in which a few adults direct a large number of pupils. He described how small-group processes, especially involving a principal as building leader and teachers as professional staff, ordinarily reach a stalemate in which any proposed change generates counterpressures. As a result, school reformers usually experience frustration as their proposals seldom affect behavioral regularities in the underlying school culture.

Nevertheless, staff development and school improvement depend on group processes and shared purposes among a building's staff or a significant subset of teachers. The importance of staff working together is implicit in Edmonds's (1982) five characteristics of effective schools: positive school leadership, agreement on goals and objectives, high expectations for students, an orderly climate, and continual monitoring and feedback on student achievement. Improved schools are possible in all kinds of communities without major changes in staffs or external conditions (Olson, 1986). Yet the school culture militates against staff working together.

COMPLEX AND CONFLICTING ROLES

A music teacher in a middle school found herself responding to adolescent concerns scarcely related to melody or harmony: "Most of the time I felt like I was a part-time child psychologist, a part-time emotional consultant. I'd have girls consulting me on whether or not they should get abortions at twelve and thirteen years old." Boys discussed "their sexual insecurities, whether this was right or that was right." Concerned about the students, she "felt that I had to deal upfront with those kids as best as I could at that time, but I didn't feel like I got much support out of the administration" (Raphael, 1985, p. 40).

Although outsiders often presume that teachers present knowledge, review central points, and then test students' understanding—in fact, teachers have to reach students where they are. Their minds are occupied by immediate personal concerns, peer pressures, and input from media as well as information and misinformation related to the formal curriculum. Yet teachers' instructional successes are measured by what their students know related to a national curriculum embodied in commercial textbooks, state and district curriculum guides, and standardized test items.

Able teachers who manage a class so as to assure adequate academic time may still find that students see few connections between Silas Marner and their own lives. For some teachers, personal priorities about world peace or ecological lifestyles may have little connection to the formal curriculum. Given the diversity of any class, teaching necessarily involves competing goals and means. Teachers make thousands of compromises each day, leaving little time to articulate or to reflect on the deeper meanings of such choices for teachers or students.

According to a recent study, teachers must combine a multiplicity of roles into their daily performance: caring; supporting; collaborating with parents; nurturing a positive learning environment; interacting in order to promote learning; researching new ideas and approaches; developing programs; planning, organizing, scheduling, assessing and communicating; and decision making/problem solving. Shirley F. Heck and C. Ray Williams (1984) summarized the characteristics needed by effective teachers in order to promote human development: "optimism about the future; authenticity; concern; belief and trust in human potential; enthusiasm; confidence; high ethical standards; willingness to admit errors; a sense of spontaneity and emotional involvement; and an innate drive to achieve" (p. 189).

Students, teachers, educational support personnel and principals face nearly incomprehensible dilemmas and ambiguities. Lieberman and Miller (1984) have sensitively described teacher behaviors as follows:

most teachers learn their roles through experience—that style emerges from work in a specific context over time. This style develops in response to major dilemmas. For the elementary teacher there are issues of:

- More subjects to teach than time to teach them
- Coverage vs. mastery

- Large-group vs. small-group instruction
- When to stay with a subject or a routine and when to shift
- How to discipline students without destroying the class
- How to deal with isolation from other adults. (p. 82)

Although teachers have considerable authority as the only adult in a roomful of young children, they are constrained by multiple responsibilities, their individual classroom and school setting, and their limited association with adults.

While secondary teachers identify more with grownups and their academic discipline, Lieberman and Miller (1984) noted bureaucratic limits on their autonomy:

For secondary teachers dilemmas are rooted in the complexity of the formal and informal system, such as:

- Personal vs. organization constraints
- Dealing with the classroom and with the whole school
- Packaging and pacing instruction to fit into allocated time periods
- Proportioning subject matter expertise and affective needs in some way
- Figuring out how to deal with mixed loyalties to the faculty and to the student culture. (p. 82)

There are enthusiastic teachers and dull teachers, motivated students and apathetic ones. Most teachers and students struggle somewhere in between. When everything clicks and lessons are clear, students are struck by new connections, insights, or clarifying knowledge. Shocks of recognition spark an electric excitement and profound understandings that are crucial for human development. More often, reading dull textbooks, homework assignments, and dogged hard work with problem sets pays off in mastery for exams or a capacity to handle detailed tasks. Sometimes, interactions among students or among teachers provide stimulus for reassessing one's values and responses to shared experiences.

Most teachers and students try, and somehow the system achieves many of its goals. Education, however, seems so massive and schools so loosely managed that no one appears in charge. According to Sarason (1982), educators "are acutely aware that they are part of a very complex arrangement of roles and functions, purposes and traditions, that are not entirely comprehensible either as a whole or in part." When they "understand" it, they regard it as irrational.

The dominant impression one gains is that school personnel believe that there is a system, that it is run by somebody or bodies in some central place, that it tends to operate as a never ending source of obstacles to those within the system, that a major goal of the individual is to protect against the baleful influences of the system, and that any one individual has and can have no effect on the system *qua* system. (p. 163)

Despite the rising importance of information management by professionals in today's society, school teachers have not developed a firm knowledge base or a sense of autonomy and status that might clarify their complex roles. They do not regard themselves as academics with appropriate salaries and responsibilities. Entry requirements are neither high nor selective, and teachers may leave and reenter or change their grade level or discipline. Working conditions are dictated by the necessity of maintaining order and safety among students whose attendance is mandatory. Teachers are accorded an ambiguous respect directed toward guardians of the young.

Complex and conflicting roles follow naturally from the variability of some 25 students. Although human beings learn in fits and starts loosely associated with stages of development related to age, students are typically divided into groups according to their year of birth. Teachers are expected to cover certain topics for all ten-year-old pupils regardless of their readiness or motivation. Responding to curricular goals determined by outside mandates and national norms, teachers experience role conflicts that foster feelings of powerlessness fundamentally at odds with their desired identity as competent and autonomous professionals.

LONELY IN A CROWDED ROOM

A beginning fourth-grade teacher recounted her own eagerness to learn—followed by a realization that colleagues seldom shared information and ideas. "Sometimes it's just: 'You do your thing in your room, and I'll do my thing in my room. Don't observe me and I don't want to observe you.' " Evaluations and informal comparisons fed competition rather than cooperation: "You're not going to get any of my ideas, and I don't want any of yours, because everybody is going to be comparing us." Her personal belief that professional development required "learning from other teachers" could not overcome school norms (Raphael, 1985, pp. 29–30).

Teaching is a lonely profession, carried out in a crowded room. Much of a teacher's felt experiences revolve around "surviving" or "coping" with some 25 active children or adolescents. Staying in control requires planned activities. Finding more or less suitable materials, adjusting them to fit some learners, responding to questions and wandering attentions, and complying with forms and public address announcements leave little time for planning daily and weekly sequences. Little wonder that teachers seldom connect their classroom discussions, questions, and lesson plans to the larger purposes of education and community development.

Over time most teachers report feeling isolated, unrespected, and unsupported as professionals. As described by Jackson (1968), Dan Lortie, and Sara Lawrence Lightfoot, even dedicated, hardworking teachers adopt a critical, wait-and-see attitude toward proposed school reforms. Lortie (1975) found that teachers developed an occupational "ethos" characterized by conservatism, a tendency to live day to day, and a sense of personal loneliness. Teacher development is "impeded by mutual isolation, vague yet demanding goals, dilemmas of outcome assessment, restricted in-service training, rigidities in assignment, and working conditions which produce a 'more-of-the-same' syndrome among classroom teachers" (p. 232). Lightfoot (1983) observed that teachers "use pet frameworks for viewing the world"; perceive change issues "autobiographically"; and focus on "what is wrong rather than search for what is right" (pp. 9–10).

Professional development depends on communication about both strengths and weaknesses as well as accurate feedback about teaching, learning and school climate. Yet teachers quickly discover that asking others, especially supervisors, for help is interpreted as evidence of inadequate performance. When outsiders visit a school they often describe staff as *"insecure, uncooperative, paranoid,* and *rigid"* (Sarason, 1982, p. 25). Outside reformers must cope "with problems that stem from the fact that the school is, in a social and professional sense, highly structured and differentiated—a fact that is related to attitudes, conceptions, and regularities of *all* who are in the setting" (Sarason, 1982, p. 49). Immersed in their school's culture, staff lack perspective to see, understand, and articulate its peculiar features.

Performing complex roles in isolation, teachers face extraordinary difficulties in explaining their roles to others. Without professional interactions, teachers often repeat what has worked previously. Their personal conservatism and loosely structured organizations reinforce routinized behaviors. Personal and social values that influence political and economic choices are seldom discussed—other than to warn teachers away from controversies. The status quo wins by default because teachers have few opportunities to share their curriculum and management plans with colleagues. Their successes go unnoted and unrewarded. School organizational patterns perpetuate isolation, teachers' power over students (and often over parents), and administrators' control of teachers' schedules and evaluations. As a consequence, many teachers resign themselves to existing patterns, complain about their salary and status, and tolerate institutional failures to deliver high quality education.

When given opportunities, however, those same teachers have enthusiastically acted to improve their instruction and their school's climate. They entered the profession because they wanted to help others to learn; and despite their frustrations with bureaucratic rules, institutional barriers to change, and uninterested colleagues, they continue to find deep personal rewards in their teaching. When partnerships between educators and outside organizations work, they stimulate crucial dialogues about curriculum, climate and educational purposes that fosters an evolving awareness by teachers of their complex professional roles.

TEACHERS' COPING STRATEGIES

Lipsky (1980) pointed to deep-seated dilemmas faced by teachers and other deliverers of human services and hence their daily struggles to devise coping strategies. Students need infinite amounts of instruction, assessment, guidance, and modeling. But for teachers, "personal and organizational resources are chronically and severely limited in relation to the tasks they must perform" (Weatherley and Lipsky, 1977, p. 3). Unable to meet every demand, teachers continually make bureaucratic decisions determining whom they serve and in what ways. Those judgments heighten the dissonance between the ideals of the helping professions and a need to routinize, ration, and otherwise cope with the literally billions of possible actions to facilitate learning in classrooms.

Unlike many professionals who provide assistance for a fee or operate within a bureaucratic organization with impersonal forms and procedures, the demand for services from street-level bureaucrats "tends to be as great as their ability to supply them" (Weatherley and Lipsky, 1977, p. 4). Teachers "work at jobs characterized by relatively high degrees of discretion and regular interaction with citizens" (Lipsky, 1980, p. 27). They make both professional judgments and bureaucratic decisions as they deliver services at no direct cost to learners. As a result, "the routines they establish, and the devices they invent to cope with uncertainties and work pressures, effectively *become* the public policies they carry out" (Lipsky, 1980, p. xii).

Street-level bureaucrats, including teachers, typically act in isolation "to salvage service and decision-making values" under adverse conditions "in a corrupted world of service" (Lipsky, 1980, p. xiii). They cope by (1) routinizing services to address groups rather than individuals, (2) modifying goals to emphasize those considered most achievable, (3) rationing services through a crude "triage" system that excludes those who need little help and those considered hopeless, (4) limiting one's clientele usually to accommodate current administrative concerns, (5) controlling students so that complaints are seldom voiced, and (6) asserting priorities suited to individual or agency strengths.

When asked, middle-school teachers who participated in the Worcester Teacher Corps project readily admitted that they used a number of tactics to implement each of the coping strategies identified by Lipsky (Bratiotis, 1982). They relied on routines, on seatwork copied or slightly modified from workbooks, on their own emphases among the broad curricular goals of their district and so on. While all teachers stifled student motivation occasionally, they credited their own good intentions somewhat more than those of their colleagues. They expressed an impression that other teachers used similar coping tactics for reasons of laziness or ignorance rather than to assert professional autonomy.

Most schools unintentionally offer disincentives for effective teaching and interactions with students. Able teachers are assigned more difficult students. Personable staff are asked to advise student groups and to chaperone evening events. Those who establish a reputation for maintaining order are assigned corridor and bus duties at difficult times or locations. Educational values seem reversed. Experienced teachers choose honors classes and relegate lower tracks to novices. School administrators make managing a safe and orderly building their primary goal, although those demands conflict with time for preparation and instruction.

From a teacher's perspective, both staff development and collaborative reforms often appear an invitation to run faster without gaining greater professional satisfaction. Sharing information about a successful lesson or new approach may engender envy rather than support. Many teachers who volunteer for leadership roles receive little peer recognition and experience a rapid "burn out" of enthusiasm. Good instructional practices are not discussed, and a tacit agreement seems to protect less successful teachers.

Since relative success generates additional demands on staff time and skills, all teachers must adopt coping strategies. That necessity makes a fair evaluation of instructional effectiveness practically impossible: all teachers routinize their day, limit student questions, and so on. When new mandates are imposed on teachers, they will predictably redirect some of their efforts; but there is little evidence that their total contributions to student development will increase. Hence, teacher improvement and overall instructional effectiveness depend primarily on teachers' willingness to seek advice and fresh ideas, to enforce both high expectations and standards cooperatively, and to build a positive climate throughout their building.

School climate suggests an ecological way of thinking about the complex ingredients of a positive learning environment. According to a standard definition, a "humane school climate" aims first "to provide throughout the school a wholesome, stimulating, and *productive* learning environment conducive to academic achievement and personal growth of youth at different levels of development" and second "to provide a pleasant and *satisfying* school situation within which young people can live and work" (Phi Delta Kappa, 1974, p. 5). In a humane school, students and staff experience respect, trust, high morale, a chance to contribute to decisions, continuous academic and social growth, a feeling of belonging, a sense of institutional renewal, and caring (pp. 7–9).

Although everyone benefits from staff agreement on instructional goals with high expectations for students, some teachers will be tempted to "freeload." They contribute little to curriculum developments or to maintaining order, but they enjoy a safe, orderly and positive climate. Because cooperation among teachers and other adults cannot be mandated, it must be fostered through leadership, administrative support, and pride in professional accomplishments. Efforts to improve effectiveness must recognize that teaching is enormously challenging—especially to meet the needs of those children who have been traditionally denied a quality education by American schools.

COMMUNICATION AND COLLEGIALITY

During the summer of 1980, university staff pondered the lessons learned from the first year of a scheduled five-year Teacher Corps project with the Worcester (Massachusetts) Public Schools (1979–1982). This university, school, and community partnership sought to improve the school learning climate for culturally diverse students from low-income neighborhoods. Next, the project planned to document information that might modify teacher development procedures in urban districts and institutions of higher education. Finally, other schools might adopt and adapt successful processes, practices and projects.

Teacher Corps guidelines and a history of joint products between the University of Massachusetts and the Worcester schools encouraged a strong effort to incorporate key research findings about staff development and school change—together with a realistic sense of feasibility. Above all, the project aimed to build on teachers' clinical expertise and involvement, as indicated by the Rand Change Agent Study (McLaughlin and Marsh, 1978). Based on a three-tiered assessment of needs and a survey of resources, a task force hammered out successive drafts of a proposal. Flow charts outlined when activities would occur. Four major outcomes were identified with objectives related to parent/community groups, teachers, the district and university, and the dissemination of successful ideas and products.

Following a year of positive achievements, evaluators noted that "we have again and again been forced to relearn that basic conditions are not transformed by a proposal and its funding" (Emery and Jones, 1980). Low-income and minority neighborhoods have seldom been well served

by schools. Declining enrollments and staff retrenchments were aggra-
vated by reductions in local revenues under a tax-capping initiative
known as Proposition 2½. Educational governance protected the en-
trenched often at the expense of teachers and programs most attuned
to the needs of students at risk. Those pressures accentuated teacher
isolation and conventional group attitudes. Professional interchanges
were guarded, filled with complaints and paranoia.

Communications had to start by recognizing these underlying forces
and conditions and then interpreting them in light of the institutional
dynamics of each setting. The district, community groups, the university, and each building had a unique history and style that implied either
strength or weakness depending on how ideas were presented. For
instance, the School of Education had a reputation for both innovation
and fragmentation. To present a credible degree program with inservice
options 50 miles away required firm commitments while preserving
some flexibility for individualized academic programs. University faculty
sought to help participants clarify and articulate their particular situation
and then to guide them through constructive planning and action within
that framework.

A myriad of details about personalities, special complications, political
connections, or previous experiences competed with messages about
overall purposes and procedures. Private conversations supplemented
general descriptions of the program because teachers had different backgrounds, needs and goals. Project coordinators distributed fact sheets
and policy statements while providing opportunities for specific questions and concerns. Individual responses bored others, and variations
among academic programs confused outsiders about the project and led
to charges of favoritism. Staff meetings and repeated clarifications
seemed the price of establishing a positive context for staff development
while adjusting to institutional and personal contexts.

Nevertheless, teachers "tested the waters" to see if they could trust
the university. Seemingly, they expected university experts and assigned
readings to provide "the answers." Teachers found "the change process
is slow and frustrating but in the end there are measurable rewards"
(Pelletz, 1979). Initially, distrust and negative attitudes prevailed.
"Teachers evidenced unknown fears: the fear of expressing their ideas
before their colleagues, the fear of reacting honestly to ideas expressed
by other colleagues, and the fear of attempting group efforts with colleagues in diverse subject areas" (Belevick and Little-Porter, 1982).

Another block to communication reflected the complexity and mag-
nitude of school change. According to later assessments by Elizabeth
Belevick and Myra Little-Porter (1982), "above all was an overwhelming
confusion concerning the purpose of our efforts and the direction we
should pursue." Brainstorming techniques helped and so did assigned

readings—especially those not directly related to teaching. Also, instructors insisted that change had to be planned in small and doable stages. Teachers often agreed on concrete steps such as writing a new discipline code when they disagreed over many other features of an improved school climate.

Dialogue with outsiders helped reconnect teacher-initiated changes and classroom behaviors to the larger purposes of an improved school climate as well as to national goals. According to the proposal for the Worcester project, four key areas defined by Teacher Corps were related to objectives developed through a series of needs assessments and surveys of resources in Worcester. Each of the four broad goals included specific project objectives connected to desired impacts and changes for the community, students and teachers, schools and the district, university policies and the broader view of educational reform:

A. IMPROVING SCHOOL LEARNING CLIMATE FOR CULTURALLY
DIVERSE STUDENTS FROM LOW INCOME NEIGHBORHOODS.

A.1 Improve communication, cooperation, and mutual support between parent/community and school staff to enhance responsiveness to diverse student needs.

A.2 Improve instructional competencies in specific areas such as basic skills, bilingual/bicultural, multicultural, individualization and team teaching through flexible, appropriate inservice and academic credit offerings to meet identified needs of students and teachers.

A.3 Develop a coherent educational plan for each project school based on needs of students, parent/community and educational personnel and the policies and goals of the district and State, and utilizing the resources of University faculty and Teacher Corps staff.

A.4 Foster ongoing articulation among the four project schools in terms of parent/community participation, student competencies, and staff development and relate that continuum to appropriate curricular areas in the School of Education. (Emery and Jones, 1982, p. 7)

During its three years of existence, teachers, interns and staff worked with teachers to strengthen the learning climate. Staff development activities fell into four major themes. Curriculum should be individualized—thus, generating learning activities packets and guidance for better use of classroom space. Parents should be involved as partners in human development—thus, producing instructional games for home use and holding sessions to familiarize parents with schools. Education should be multicultural—thus, emphasizing Worcester's rich ethnic heritage and its growing Hispanic population. Positive supervision should build school improvements into normal patterns of teacher interactions—thus, suggesting a new approach to evaluation.

When the project ended earlier than anticipated due to funding cuts, most active participants believed that their involvement had led to school improvements. Teachers' comments reflected a functional understanding of how their efforts had promoted a positive climate for learning: "The first visible sign of change was the recognition of a common goal, that being to work together for change." Belevick and Little-Porter (1982) had observed the impact of communication among teachers:

Within the school working together has led to a cohesiveness that was not previously observable. There has been more sharing of ideas, more willingness to help each other, and even more socializing, an important factor in gaining understanding of one's colleagues. Working together on projects for the school has also led to mutual pride in accomplishment, giving us still more in common.

Major lessons were learned about communication and collegiality:

1. discuss conditions and prospects in realistic terms;
2. rephrase criticisms of others to reflect personal concerns of teachers;
3. allow time to build trust;
4. develop skills for sharing ideas;
5. alter institutional communication patterns, particularly by adjusting bureaucratic forms and deadlines to fit with lives of teachers;
6. separate activities into bite-sized pieces in order to enhance feasibility;
7. start with familiar ideas and then mix in diverse insights;
8. encourage efficient use of teacher time by supporting a center rich in resources with equipment to duplicate materials; and
9. relate the parts to the whole and achievements to purposes;

Change requires involvement by many individuals in a school, creating and sharing both activities and meanings that relate to the needs, personalities, and climate of a particular building.

EMPOWERING TEACHERS TO COLLABORATE

The Worcester project illustrated that new patterns of school climate and formal curriculum emerge only when sustained by a critical mass of teachers with support from parents and administrators. Being right and self-righteously isolated is little better than being wrong. School change advocates have learned not to insist that teachers adopt innovations as mandated by an outside agency or a curriculum specialist. Given an organizational framework and support, teachers in Worcester welcomed opportunities to escape from isolation, to share their frustrations in complex roles, and to help shape their school's purposes and expectations.

Both in person and in research literature, teachers present a dual view of their role and that ambiguity confuses professional development. "As one's vision expands beyond the interactions of teachers and children within classrooms," Lightfoot has noted, "the image of the teacher as an autonomous, powerful, and central figure changes. Within the broader contexts of school systems, communities, and occupational structures, teachers tend to be described as powerless, isolated, and subordinate" (Carew and Lightfoot, 1979, p. 17). Many adults who seek to collaborate with schools recall a classroom experience with a dominating teacher and then discover an insecure professional—isolated from other adults, operating from a knowledge base that is limited, and unsure about how her or his teaching produces learning.

Collaborations that improve schools for students must modify existing teacher and student interactions. According to Sarason's summary, programmatic and behavioral regularities should have predictable outcomes that are measurable and desired. Yet educators can demonstrate few consistent relationships between school inputs and student learning. Most proposed reforms affect only a small part of what happens in schools. "In practice, the regularities tend not to be changed and the intended outcomes, therefore, cannot occur; that is, the more things change the more they remain the same" (Sarason, 1982, p. 116).

Although teachers and other support staff often feel powerless, schools are intensely political organizations. Most teachers have uneasily adjusted to a complex setting and its perceived distribution of clout and respect. Any innovation threatens someone's sense of prestige. Modifying existing behaviors, introducing new programs, or involving other participants all generate resistance from those who are comfortable with old ways and existing distributions of authority. "Introducing, sustaining, and assessing an educational change are political processes because they inevitably alter or threaten to alter existing power relationships, especially if that process implies, as it almost always does, a reallocation of resources" (Sarason, 1982, p. 71).

For teachers and administrators, the key distributions of authority and status are within the school system. Often staff development activities encouraged the development of new leadership cadres among teachers. In Worcester, Teacher Corps participants viewed themselves as "generally younger, more optimistic, more enthusiastic," according to Belevick and Little-Porter (1982). "There is some jealousy among the uninvolved, a questioning of why certain people, formerly in the background of school leadership, now function in the forefront. The key answer is involvement; many individuals on becoming more involved have broadened their scope of leadership within the school tremendously."

If partnerships offer new resources and perspectives that foster school improvements, they will alter power balances. Seldom will parents, business leaders, other human service professionals, and university faculty agree on what should be done. As a result, collaborations may expand a political struggle with uncertain consequences for school systems. Further, issues of power—and issues of control over one's life—are intimately connected with definitions of teachers as professionals who must continually reestablish their minimum standards and acceptable behaviors, their credentials and standard practices.

We argue that partnerships can reverse some of the forces affecting teachers, school climates and professional development. For changes to be implemented, teachers have to buy into a proposed innovation, participate in its adoption and adaptation, and modify basic regularities in their school's culture. Reformers must willingly give up yesterday's plans and improvements to reconceptualize fresh ways to respond to the needs of students, parents, and their community. Sustained school improvements are those that become embedded in ordinary goals and behaviors of a school's staff. Epistemological and social science insights, discussed in the next chapter, may suggest a metaframework for reexamining common problems, processes and potentials of partnerships.

3
Understanding School Partnerships

Imagine an extraterrestrial visitor (ETV) who lands at a baseball game—or a public school. ETV "observes" countless movements and interactions by "humans." Over time individuals appear, move about, act, handle objects, talk with and touch each other, and then leave; but the meaning of their performances is baffling. Nevertheless, ETV assumes that humans function with knowledge and a sense of purpose so that predictable outcomes will follow from repeated behaviors.

During the warmer parts of the year, for example, human beings gather inside a large enclosure labeled "Yankee Stadium." Soon a number of individuals dressed in uniform outfits move about on an oddly shaped green space using sticks and gloves to handle a small round object. Meanwhile, other persons sit in the surrounding areas. They make loud noises with their hands, imbibe liquids through their mouths, and occasionally toss things resembling small flying saucers. Varied patterns are illuminated on a portion of the outer boundaries. After about three hours everyone leaves—some happily, some dejectedly.

The public and private purposes of this activity are mysterious to the visitor. Is the meaning revealed in the bleachers or on the field? Do the crowds attract the players to perform or do people come to watch some planned actions? Only after learning baseball from the "inside," as it is experienced and understood by players and fans alike, will ETV understand the focus, rules, outcomes, and satisfactions of the game. If ETV had experienced team sports or spectator events, some observations may seem explicable. Nonetheless, several plausible hypotheses "explain" major league players' obsession with home plate without clarifying that the batter seeks to hit the ball within a certain quadrant but out of the reach of any fielder.

Landing at a school, ETV would find similarly bewildering interpersonal and organizational patterns. An adult (usually a male, but seldom wearing a white shirt or a necktie) arrives first, leaves last, has the most keys, and does things in every room in the building. ETV might well view the "custodian" as the organization's most important person. Day after day, bells and public address announcements occur at intervals, signaling new activities. Many younger persons enter, talk, move about, read and write, and take part in games while an older individual periodically offers different responses. Reasons for these actions are unclear to a visitor from outer space, nor are they necessarily obvious to many inhabitants of the planet Earth. Confusion will persist till ETV learns what people in schools take for granted when they refer to "students," "teachers," and "learning."

SOCIALLY CONSTRUCTED MEANINGS

According to Alfred Schutz's studies of phenomenology in the 1940s and 1950s, individuals construct reality through their perception of day-to-day meetings, conversations, and relationships among people. Schutz (1962, 1964, 1967) described how individuals construct personal meanings in light of their social experiences and then act according to those understandings. A first time visitor to a ball game quite simply has a different experience from that of a player or an avid fan. This belief that individuals create meaning for their lives is known as *constructivism* in developmental psychology (Piaget, 1965, 1968; Kegan, 1982; Gilligan, 1982; Fingarette, 1963) or *reality construction* in interpretive or phenomenological sociology (Schutz, 1967; Berger and Luckmann, 1967; Garfinkel, 1967).

In phenomenological terms, social reality is not a unitary, fixed, or known-in-advance set of ideas or facts, accessible to all social actors. As McHugh (1968) suggested:

If observations differ according to time and place of measurement, there is no possibility of a physical or social ontology. There are instead multiple realities— valid through varied descriptions of a set of relationships that depend upon one's perspective or location within the set. (p. 29)

For example, the statement "I am going to school" by a fifteen-year-old American youth is rich with socially derived meanings. That same announcement by someone who is five, thirty-five, or seventy-five has a dramatically different meaning.

In order to communicate and interact with others, individuals assume "reciprocity of perspectives and interchangeability of standpoints" (Schutz and Luckmann, 1973, p. 60). Individuals assume that if they were in the other's place, they would experience everyday situations from the other's perspective—and vice versa. As in the case of traffic accident reports, there are overlapping contexts of agreement and disagreement about details of an event. Presumably, an underlying reality exists that is somehow misperceived by some citizens, which accounts for multiple responses. Schutz insisted, however, that individuals construct their own meanings and act accordingly within the limits of their experiences.

In his essay on "The Stranger" (1964; originally published in 1944), Schutz contrasted routine, business-as-usual behaviors of an established group with problems of orientation and adaptation faced by immigrants and other outsiders. A "member of the in-group looks in a single glance through the normal social situations occurring to him and . . . he catches immediately the ready-made recipe appropriate to its solution. In those situations his acting shows all the marks of habituality, automatism, and half-consciousness" (p. 101).

A stranger, Schutz (1964) noted, lacks a "ready-made standardized scheme of the cultural pattern" that can serve as an "unquestioned and unquestionable guide in all the situations" (p. 95). Trying to understand unfamiliar rules, an outsider brings a different objectivity to a new setting:

The deeper reason for his objectivity, however, lies in his own bitter experience of the limits of the "thinking as usual". . . . Therefore, the stranger discerns, frequently with a grievous clear-sightedness, the rising of a crisis which may menace the whole foundation of the "relatively natural conception of the world," while all those symptoms pass unnoticed by the members of the in-group . . . . (p. 104)

In most organizations, members interact without major discrepancies among important individual constructions about the meaning of group life. That is, a principal behaves like a principal and a student like a student. Therefore, teachers presume regular responses to everyday actions from each. Schutz's "reciprocity of perspectives" and "interchangeability of standpoints" allow individuals to explain away contradictory evidence. Such assumptions and knowledge about functional roles are essential for purposeful actions. Accordingly, individual understandings are continually adjusted to correspond with evolving social meanings.

Nevertheless, individual understandings of common events vary enormously so that communication is complex and often misinterpreted. Hence, within functioning organizations, common meanings are assumed and "enforced" through behavioral regularities. As members of organizations or social groups, participants act as if rules or events mean the same to everyone. When differences arise, they are often dealt with by attributing a particular willfulness or careless misinterpretation to other persons. Or members may choose to ignore discrepancies in favor of what are assumed to be ideas and perspectives held in common. They "take it for granted that whoever is listening to their communications will know all of what they mean even when they use only indirect or very partial references to that meaning" (Douglas, 1974, p. 115).

In certain interpersonal and organizational situations, particular realities dominate through power relationships. For instance, drill sergeants inform recruits that there is a right way, a wrong way, and the army's way. The military can then act as though every training exercise and order makes sense—while individuals retain doubts as to the meaningfulness of "hurry up and wait" procedures. Schools, like the army, function on well-understood patterns that almost everyone accepts. Preschool-age children are frequently baffled by expectations that students behave "properly" and not question authority (Paley, 1981). When secondary teachers have defined their roles as facilitative and supportive rather than directive or punitive, they confused their adolescent students (Dennison, 1969).

Constructivism has implications for the language used to depict human development and learning in schools. Carol Gilligan (1977) described that larger framework:

> The revolutionary contribution of Piaget's work is the experimental confirmation and refinement of Kant's assertion that knowledge is actively constructed rather than passively received. Time, space, self, and other, as well as the categories of development theory, all arise out of the active interchange between the individual and the physical and social world in which he lives and of which he strives to make sense. The development of cognition is the process of reappropriating reality at progressively more complex levels of apprehension, as the structures of thinking expand to encompass the increasing richness and intricacy of experience. (p. 483)

From a perspective of phenomenological sociology, schooling involves a massive effort to create a common reality for a society. Ways of understanding, acting, interacting and communicating are learned and reinforced. As a result, males and females, young and old, Black and White can discuss and react to a range of at least nominally shared historical and cultural events. Accordingly, certain "objects" become important: the American flag, the story of the Civil War, the gross national product, principles of social tolerance, and the Golden Rule. Because a "social heritage" that defines "relevances and typifications" (Schutz and Luckmann, 1973, p. 237) is taken as objective reality, it obscures the radical individualism of phenomenology and thereby conceals the personal and social processes of constructed meanings.

CONCEPTS FOR UNDERSTANDING COLLABORATIONS

We have adopted three broad concepts from social sciences that illuminate common experiences of school people and their partners in school improvement: *multiple realities, ill-structured problems,* and *reflexive thinking.* From a phenomenological perspective, people experience interorganizational activities in terms of their individual meaning systems. The resulting multiple realities of collaboration may either disrupt cooperative programs or promote a rethinking of educational purposes. Typically, schools welcome partners when standard educational problems no longer yield satisfactory solutions. By defining problems in ill-structured terms, people can envision alternative resolutions. Then, individuals and organizations may evolve new understandings about themselves in their settings through reflexive thinking.

Multiple realities, ill-structured problems, and reflexivity identify common dynamics present in interorganizational collaborations. When teachers and their partners view the daily realities of schools in different terms, their individual experiences open fresh ways to see schools and education. In so doing, they connect personalities, scenarios, and unfolding dramas to analytical frameworks that make processes of change understandable and manageable. These multidisciplinary perspectives allow a triangulation for identifying, validating, and then understanding common processes (Patton, 1980, pp. 108–9). Throughout, we use these concepts to understand causes, to describe processes, and to comprehend outcomes of partnerships.

These key concepts form a pattern of analytic relationships that illuminate interorganizational dynamics:

1. Individuals in organizations continually construct and reconstruct their understandings of daily experience and their perceptions of associates. According to constructivism, an individual's occupation and related everyday experiences shape her or his reality. In complex organizations like elementary and secondary schools, an interplay of selves and settings sustains individual multiple realities and institutional cultures.

2. In the absence of compelling contrary evidence, individuals assume that their understandings of reality are shared and satisfactory accounts of events. Most individuals function within a constrained environment of family, neighborhood, and work, where "local knowledge" is both sufficient and functional. Universal schooling is followed by common economic and political experiences that allow individuals to speak and act in a wider social world.

3. Daily life is organized around repeated behaviors or regularities giving rise to public vocabularies and scripts. These regularities, however, may hold somewhat different meanings for individuals in subparts of an organization or those with a different institutional framework. Thus, multiple but non-

conflicting realities characterize normal organizational interactions and problem solving.

4. Within established institutions, multiple realities usually pass unnoticed till external shifts or internal developments threaten personal assumptions and/or organizational regularities. When members sense something is amiss but no standard response seems appropriate, then problems become ill-structured.

5. When routine reactions fail to resolve a perceived problem, deep disagreements about meanings raise issues for organizational strategies and structures. Individuals and organizational subunits respond unpredictably to puzzles and anomalies outside their groups' constructed rules.

6. Individual and organizational efforts to resolve ill-structured problems may either insistently maintain the status quo or transcend these anomalies by generating new personal assumptions and organizational regularities. Collaborative governance and substructures may create an arena for considering ill-structured problems without interfering with basic organizational patterns.

7. Evolving understandings for individuals and organizations follow from new activities and modified psychological meaning systems. Ordinarily, different activities shape attitudes or beliefs that affect behaviors; and, in turn, those attitudes suggest alternative organizational strategies or purposes implemented through new structures.

8. As patterns emerge, individuals and organizations can self-consciously sense their own evolving understanding of their work lives and the social world. Involvement in partnerships enables one to experience different organizational frameworks that encourage reflection and reconstruction of individual or group perspectives.

9. As partnerships evolve, reflexive thinking helps participants use their formal and informal knowledge to devise organizational structures that affect school experiences for students, staffs, and outside collaborators.

MULTIPLE REALITIES

While observing and participating in partnerships during the past decade, we have at times felt like ETVs struggling to understand interpersonal and organizational patterns of schools. As strangers to the embedded beliefs, local knowledge, and daily relationships of insiders, we often were puzzled about the meanings of our observations. For example, we had few clues about social hierarchies among students that are manifested in adolescent styles and fads. Unfamiliar with established norms, we encouraged teachers in one school to open communication with their colleagues only to learn that some felt they had violated the gender segregation prevailing in their staff lounge.

As members of organizations interact, they "fill in" their conservations with taken-for-granted assumptions. Thus, elementary teachers who are responsible for a classroom of 25 to 30 children cannot explain to outsiders the intensity and complexity of their roles. Within a high school, teachers of biology and history seldom discuss curriculum outside their own departmental or professional meetings. Principals who stress a safe and orderly environment may worry more about hall-duty assignments than instructional leadership. Educators, like family members or plumbers, readily engage in dialogue and cooperative activities—although many of their scenarios baffle casual observers.

Individuals follow embedded scripts and stage directions that have been assembled through experiencing particular settings. Most Americans recall their days in school and assume they understand what happens there. Yet students experience classrooms far differently from teachers and administrators. Oddly, most adults know too much about schools, just as ETV knows too little, for teachers to discuss the dilemmas of their professional roles. Perhaps a visiting educator from Australia would elicit the clearest explanation of American schools. Nevertheless, adults—whose classroom experiences are often decades as well as miles apart—presume a shared vocabulary about education.

Embedded in people's notions about schools are activities and relationships that define educational reforms. Both insiders and outsiders enter collaborative relationships through their own perspectives and vocabularies, and they are relatively unprepared for the scripts of others. Parents, business leaders, human service professionals, or university staffs seldom understand the pressures on teachers. As a result, discussions and common activities give rise to diverse understandings of school purposes, processes, structures, and climates. Over time, agreements on change strategies may follow from both sensitivity to multiple realities and some common experiences.

School partnerships raise issues of interpretation among individuals and between organizations. For example, during interchanges between parent organizations and teachers, many parents arrive with a feeling that schools have failed to address the needs of their children. On the other hand, teachers contend that parents have not prepared children appropriately for classroom routines. Separately, each group may reinforce its own viewpoint while agreeing that working together is important. Collectively, they face numerous difficulties in sustaining joint activities. Each has derived separate agendas from their personal and organizational experiences.

Parents and teachers—as well as other groups—work together successfully in many situations. Parent/school advisory councils may be mandated by federal regulations; they may establish a mutual exchange of services, as when both groups resist closing a neighborhood school; or they may cooperate on limited matters, such as a fund-raising drive to support an athletic team or band. Multiple realities appear disruptive when these interchanges extend beyond ordinary assumptions and expectations. Voluntary partnerships almost inevitably raise questions of whose point of view will prevail or whose social construction of reality will be maintained.

When ideas about planning, time frames, role definitions, and other aspects of cooperation differ greatly, members of organizations face both personal and institutional dilemmas. They must explain how persons who are apparently viewing the same events can describe them in disparate and contradictory ways. When there is disillusionment or conflict in partnerships, individuals struggle to determine what really happened and how the other partner arrived at a conflicting version. They may conclude that other individuals lack a sincere desire for educational reform.

For partners, a real possibility exists that those involved, lacking mutually understood perspectives, will be unable to continue working together. Those uncertainties or disagreements repeatedly appear when cooperative projects break down or lose momentum. Differences, once raised, must be resolved. Otherwise, "further purposive interaction becomes difficult, if not impossible, because much of the basis of common, everyday assumptions from which such interaction proceeds has been removed" (Filmer et al., 1972, p. 223).

Although multiple realities have proven to be a weakness in some partnerships (Maloy, 1985; Sarason, 1982; Trubowitz et al., 1984), we believe they can be transformed into a major strength. Collaborations seldom flourish without some understanding of how organizational cultures shape the experiences of participants. Partners have different agendas, interests and dreams; yet they choose to work together. Different norms and expectations can be created by organizational experiences so that partners construct a common vocabulary.

ILL-STRUCTURED PROBLEMS

Most issues can be stated in well-structured terms by adults within a framework of known and predictable responses. Organizations exist to bring efficiency to large-scale projects by coordinating a series of repeated activities toward a planned goal. Ordinarily a problem is diagnosed and a remedy prescribed. For example, children with academic problems are evaluated, an individual educational plan is developed, and then it is implemented in accordance with Public Law 94–142, which requires mainstreaming or maximal placement in regular classrooms for children with special needs. That response, however, does not question whether all educational settings are too restrictive or whether the curriculum meets any student's real needs.

Teachers generally organize lessons around well-structured problems.

"They are problems in solution, often, in name only," Mitroff (1983) wrote. The text or teacher provides a question and the requisite information for a solution. "The student's problem is to apply the right principles in the right sequence to derive a correct or optimal answer to the given problem" (p. 164). Questions with ambiguous or unclear answers are not treated seriously. Mitroff described such puzzles as ill-structured problems. People (and school systems) prefer well-structured problems and tend to ignore complex or fuzzy social and educational issues. Teachers are asked how and when to cover a subject but are seldom asked what students should know and why.

Ill-structured problems raise issues of multiple realities, as Mitroff (1983) noted. "Ill-structured problems not only vary in their definitions from stakeholder to stakeholder; they vary over time as well. They are dynamic. A solution for one time period and one set of conditions is not necessarily a solution for another." No scientific study can conclusively resolve such issues: " . . . there are either too many or too few data, never exactly the right amount of the right kind" (pp. 165, 166). Both conclusions and methodology are subject to challenges. No one, Mitroff insisted, should scoff at "reinventing the wheel" when members seek a possible solution for a poorly defined problem.

Well-specified reforms minimize ill-structuredness; but in so doing, they shape how innovations are conceptualized. For instance, a small group of teachers, administrators, and parents volunteered to prepare a handbook of community-based resources for families and children in their district—as required by P.L. 94–142. They agreed to compile a comprehensive listing of agencies and services—modeled after a resource guide from a neighboring district. The group divided the tasks of contacting local agencies to obtain current information.

Shortly thereafter, an outsider listened to the group's progress report and its complaints about lack of time and cooperation. He suggested that the group had misinterpreted its goal by organizing themselves to complete the handbook—without considering how school and community people might use information about outside resources. His observation generated a "shock of reinvention" among the members of the group. They had ignored the quality and accessibility of services. They had not considered that parents might find a geographic or functional arrangement of social agencies more helpful than an alphabetical listing.

Insiders regularly recognize well-structured problems that imply their own solution and seldom modify behavioral regularities. On the other hand, outsiders add elements of ill-structuredness to educational reform. Differing organizational perspectives may bring new ways of understanding the complexities of school cultures and conceptualizing change. Broader social concerns or longer time-horizons can alter problem definitions. Potential solutions from other settings can be tried. For example, school administrators ordinarily employ only certified staff; but laypersons readily suggest that lawyers, musicians, potters or authors might also teach.

According to organizational theorist William Torbert (1976), there are benefits to be gained from focusing on ill-structured problems. Normal institutional arrangements "focus on doing the predefined task"; "in which standards and structures are taken for granted"; which emphasize "quantitative results based on defined standards"; and in which "reality is conceived as dichotomous and competitive." Less structured organizations or collaborations could share "reflection about larger (wider, deeper, more long-term, more abstract) purposes," develop an "open interpersonal process, with disclosure, support, and confrontation on value-stylistic-emotional issues"; evaluate "the efforts of one's own behavior on others in the organization"; assess "the effects of the organization on the environment"; and openly discuss central issues of authority and participation, traditional values and future adaptations (pp. 158–59).

In school partnerships, the scale of change may be tipped in one of two directions: either the presence of ill-structured problems will undermine cooperation through the interplay of various perspectives or those differences will generate fresh, critical ideas that support substantive improvements in the organizational patterns of schools. When partners begin with a sense of mutual trust or a strong desire to work together, they can tolerate ambiguities arising from multiple visions of school improvement. A flexible collaborative arrangement can incorporate ill-structured problem solving without revamping basic organizational systems.

REFLEXIVE THINKING

Reflexive thinking involves a self-consciousness about one's perspectives that leads to shifts in how one perceives herself or himself in the world. Understandings evolve when individuals or organizations change their ways of interpreting the world and gain perspective on where they are or have been. This is called a "transformation" by Robert Kegan and other developmental psychologists. For example, "the typical four-year-old child has a host of original and (to our minds) amusingly strange views about nature" (Keagan, 1982, p. 26). The child may believe the moon follows people when they walk or that tall, thin beakers contain more water than short, wide beakers (as in Piaget's classic experiment). Using these perceptions and impulses, the child cannot comprehend certain things about the way older siblings or parents think and act.

The dramatic transformations associated with childhood and adolescence occur during adulthood as well. As human beings mature, they emerge from a "psychological evolutionary state" and "from embeddedness in a particular human context" (Kegan, 1982, p. 257) while gaining perspective on their own and others' growth. At every stage or "evolutionary truce," individuals maintain a meaning system whose integrity imposes order on their values and actions. As they achieve a capacity for perspective-taking, they examine and change their assumptions and behaviors. Kegan (1982, p. 109) depicted a spiral of human development (see Figure 3.1).

Infants identify the self with their parents or other important adults. In early childhood, impulsiveness is embedded in self without considering the perspectives of others. A capacity to separate one's own (imperial) point of view from the point of view of others develops from childhood to adolescence. A youth's sense of self is typically defined interpersonally, particularly in terms of friends and peers. Adults often associate their identity with their institutional roles—librarian, citizen,

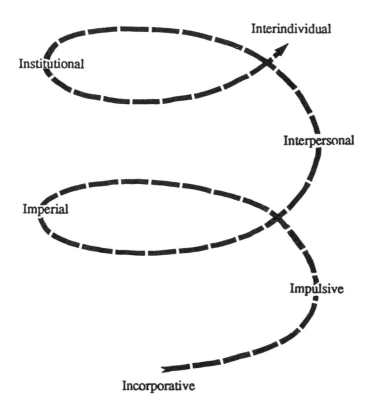

Figure 3.1
A Helix of Evolutionary Truces

parent, Unitarian, and bridge player. Mature adults move toward greater personal autonomy associated with particular ideas and values that incorporate, but are not dependent on, the influence of other people or organizations.

At each stage, adults see others and their organizational roles in different ways, as in Kegan and Lahey's (1984) illustration of how three teachers viewed their principal. One believed that the principal regarded them as employees rather than as persons (an interpersonal frame). Another teacher saw an accessible leader and personal friend who gave feedback in a helpful manner (an institutional frame). A third teacher described the principal as a valued colleague and like-minded thinker who looked out for teachers as professionals (an interindividual frame). "Of course, each is talking about the same physical entity, but if each is constructing reality out of a whole different logic, then in the psychological sense three different 'objects' do exist . . . " (p. 211).

Adults may not evolve through all stages during their lifetime, and rates of development vary, as Kegan noted. Some adults shift back and forth between interpersonal and institutional stages—valuing family and friends as much as their professional commitments. Some teachers identify so completely with their classroom that they devote 70 to 90 hours a week to work and regard student failures as a proof of their personal inadequacies. Some educators achieve a rare balance of institutional goals and social ethics with personal ambitions and values. Ordinarily, adults move to a new evolutionary truce after some personal or professional situation that requires major readjustments—starting a family enforces a career orientation or a heart attack reminds one that life holds more than work and worry.

Predictably, educators who are at varying stages of adult development produce conflicting signals. Although teaching historically attracted many who wanted to help others, it has not developed the same professional loyalty exhibited by lawyers or research chemists. Because effective instruction generates student curiosity, teaching becomes an absorbing commitment for many dedicated practitioners. Hence, those who are most identified with making schools work—teachers who design new curriculum, work with students, seek to improve test scores, and fight for higher professional standards—seldom view the strengths and weaknesses of their school from an interindividual perspective. Teachers at an interindividual stage balance personal goals, standards of excellent instruction, and a sense of larger educational purposes.

Although organizational cultures make the work environment predictable to both insiders and outsiders, those patterns discourage reflection and organizational self-consciousness. Often a major institutional crisis is required to reshape perspectives and induce change. As Deal and Kennedy (1982) suggested, change agents can reshape an organization's ethos if they "deliberately attack the problem in a way that makes people in the culture sit up and say 'What in the world is going on here?' Only in this way will real changes in the behavior of people be achieved throughout the organization" (p. 150). Typically, changes evolve in unanticipated directions with new understandings.

Partnerships can introduce different perspectives, allow individuals to explore new approaches, and generate alternative organizational strategies and substructures—all without requiring a major shakeup of the institution. By bringing multiple realities and ill-structured problems within loosely connected organizational frameworks, partnerships encourage reflexive thinking that is appropriate for adult development. Furthermore, school partnerships benefit from those individuals who have achieved mature professional skills and are ready to reflect on how schools should contribute to social and economic developments.

EQUITY IN COLLABORATIONS

Equity and fairness of educational services are important (although often overlooked) issues in school improvement collaborations. Many recent partnerships have been initiated or supported by public mandates, judicial decisions, or outside funds intended to compensate for recognized inequities affecting students. Also, outside resources have been sought by those schools and districts with demonstrable needs. Instructional innovations and alternative structures fostered by partnerships can help students who are poorly educated, involve teachers who are currently alienated, and aid schools now contributing little to community development. Unless partnerships augment fairness through a new mission, resources, and roles, they will not realize their potential.

Fairness carries many implications for school improvement. If partnerships merely assist those who already have an advantaged position, they perpetuate win-lose contests. Standardized curriculum and tests have rank-ordered students quite effectively for half a century. Once hierarchies are established and connected to educational credentials, then knowledge is less important than the prestige of one's degrees. Helping advantaged students and schools offers few incentives for extra effort since relative social status will remain unchanged.

Successful change may be as simple as shifting from norm-referenced to criterion-referenced standards—or pragmatically downplaying assessments of outcomes that reflect achievement and emphasizing instead fairness of instruction. Because only a minority of students, teachers, schools, or districts can be clearly above average, much outside pressure for improved schools strikes its intended audience as an invitation to run faster in order to maintain one's relative position. Too often, intended rewards translate into additional tasks. Students take "enrichment" courses, teachers pursue advanced degrees, principals encourage parent participation; but social hierarchies remain unchanged. Improvements in one school become a challenge to others to catch up rather than achievements to be savored.

Typical group interactions suggest another reason for emphasizing fairer outcomes. A normal cycle of development is well known: a group selects a leader and then criticizes that individual till she or he quits. Next, the group identifies a new leader and repeats the process till no one willingly accepts a leadership role. As long as group processes proceed in this manner, reforms will be self-limiting. Assuming the "system" cannot be altered, teachers view change in terms of personalities or political tactics. From this standpoint, collaborations become perceived as a process in which some gain and others lose (perhaps only places in a presumed queue awaiting promotion). They generate conflicts or reasons for nonparticipation by those not well-situated to benefit from proposed reforms.

Finally, schools have to respond to a world with far readier access to media and information than in earlier times. "Children of the post–World War II decades came to school prepared to be active and stimulated in relation to a world of fascinating possibilities, not to a world of schooling that was *obviously* unconnected to a world they saw and heard about elsewhere" (Sarason, 1983, p. 104). Collaborations that are designed to improve learning outcomes for students must avoid simply reinforcing a "made up" curriculum to which students seldom relate. "The child has self-interests in the sense that he or she seeks knowledge and skills to achieve a sense of mastery and self-worth, and this seeking should be both encouraged by and protected through schooling" (Sarason, 1983, p. 172).

If partnerships merely reinforce existing organizational regularities and patterns of inequity, then their potential as a school improvement tactic will go largely untapped. When prosperous businesses contribute funds to reward high achievers or when universities offer traditional academic courses for inservice training, fundamental patterns of schools remain unaffected. Alternatively, we envision situations where school people, sharing a sense of mutual growth through connections with outside groups, can gain the knowledge and power needed to promote equity for students, teachers and schools.

TOWARD UNDERSTANDING COLLABORATIVE ACTIVITIES

Given their conflicting roles and isolation, educators need time and space to reconsider their roles and purposes. A number of school-based projects have adopted some variation of a "minisabbatical," as described by the staff development director in Worcester (Durkin, 1975). In essence, school staff are released during the week or take time over a weekend to visit another site for both structured activities and informal discussions. Minisabbaticals enabled Worcester teachers to "conceptualize a new program and prepare a proposal for consideration by school administrators" (Miller and Wolf, 1978, p. 152). Those events combined aspects of a retreat, professional conference, workshop, and social gathering.

Between 1981 and 1985, regular minisabbatical weekends attracted about 150 educators from BSSP, Roosevelt, Worcester Teacher Corps, MESTEP, and other collaborations to the Amherst campus of the University of Massachusetts. For instance, in October 1983 teachers, administrators, and university faculty gathered at the Campus Center on Friday afternoon. Professor Harvey Scribner, former Chancellor of the New York City Public Schools, discussed national reports on education reform. In a keynote address, State Representative James Collins, Cochair of the Joint Committee on Education in Massachusetts, offered his assessment of public schools. The session concluded with a wine and cheese reception. On Saturday morning, concurrent seminars were facilitated by faculty and staff on topics such as research methodology, library resources, professional writing, career transition and renewal, and stress management. Saturday afternoon allowed "program specific time" for class meetings, academic advising, planning school improvement activities, and informal interactions.

Evaluations confirmed that participants appreciated the "timeout" from the pressures of the day-to-day world (Maloy and Seldin, 1984). They found opportunities to consider significant issues during the formal sessions while meeting other educators and old associates. Feelings of personal isolation and disconnectedness were replaced by a renewed sense of involvement and support. University faculty and staff learned from school-based improvement teams and discovered connections between research results and teachers' daily experiences.

Multiple realities, ill-structured problems, and reflexive thinking helped us to understand how and why minisabbaticals functioned effectively as cause, as process, and as outcomes. Minisabbaticals responded to teacher isolation and powerlessness reflecting multiple realities. Multiple realities also described what happened when practitioners journeyed to a new site, juxtaposed ideas, and discussed change projects with colleagues. Finally, multiple realities illuminated the significance of minisabbaticals and other collaborative efforts that promoted new insights and understandings.

Similarly, because members of educational organizations viewed problems in well-structured terms, meetings among several groups helped those who participated to expand problem definitions. As groups become more familiar with brainstorming to elicit information from one another, activities and discussions became less well-structured and often more productive. For example, administrators tended to dominate the initial minisabbaticals, but over time teachers asserted their own ideas. Procedurally, schedules for activities that were tightly arranged became more flexible as individuals learned to tolerate ambiguity and fuzzy processes. Thus, outcomes for partnerships can be understood in terms of creating alternative problem definitions.

An underlying rationale for sabbaticals, whatever their format, is to allow time for reflection. A different scene with a different mix of people, perspectives, and problems invites some reconsideration of one's role in a professional setting. In many cases, participants learned that their dilemmas were present elsewhere and thus in all probability were not caused by the personal and political factors ordinarily blamed for problems. Ideally, these new perspectives enable educators to return to their building with fresh ideas for unblocking political stalemates.

Equity adds new layers to assessments of collaborative efforts, including minisabbaticals, by focusing attention on school change that redistributes power. Much of the literature about school change has condemned the status quo without much regard for the direction of change. All those who are dissatisfied can agree schools should be changed without having to agree on means or ends. Planners of collaborative projects should propose ways to empower teachers. Discussions should involve input from elementary teachers, beginning teachers, parents, students and others usually passed over. Programs should enhance learning opportunities for students who are currently underserved and activities should open leadership roles for women and minorities.

Although collaborative interactions can be described in terms of the concepts discussed in this chapter, each by itself misses elements of crucial scenarios and outcomes. Taken collectively, the ideas enrich each other and account for interactive processes within collaborations. As we study partnerships in greater detail, multiple realities, ill-structured problems, reflexivity, and equity strengthen an understanding of developmental stages and activities.

PART TWO

STUDIES OF PARTNERSHIPS

4

A School District and a
University

In August 1982, the Roosevelt Union Free School District on Long Island entered into an agreement for a staff development partnership with the University of Massachusetts at Amherst. In a one-year contract calling for a payment of $16,445, the School of Education agreed to offer appropriate courses for Roosevelt teachers and administrators who were interested in school improvement. Class sessions would be scheduled Friday evenings and Saturdays in Amherst; and Roosevelt staff might earn advanced degrees, including an Ed.D., through individualized academic programs. University faculty would visit the district for two days during each semester in order to link change strategies to district needs and possibilities. Their presentations would be open to staff members as part of the district's normal inservice programs.

The contract has been renewed five times. Based on a description of project goals and achievements, the American Association of School Administrators selected the Roosevelt/University of Massachusetts collaboration as an Exemplary Staff Development Model (see brief description in *School Administrator*, 1985). The project aimed at improving student achievement through staff-initiated school projects supported by an active partnership with a large university located 190 miles away in another state.

The Roosevelt/University of Massachusetts Staff Development Project exemplified good collaborative practices between schools and outside organizations. Starting with an exchange of people and resources between a school system and an outside organization, the partnership nurtured and sustained mutual learning processes. As participants experienced new activities and settings, both teachers and faculty shared multiple realities and fresh possibilities. New ways of thinking about education emerged, giving rise to additional cooperative activities both within the schools and between Roosevelt and the University in Amherst.

Most partnerships develop through several phases marked by multilayered negotiations, shifting interests, agreements on activities or ends, and personal leadership within a framework of possibilities established by the purposes, capabilities, cultures, and personalities of the collaborating organizations. This case study demonstrates how partnerships can support teacher development and school improvement. It describes the actions and interactions for sharing means and goals, analyzes the dynamics of change, and clarifies how new understandings and capacities can be learned by participants. Detailed analyses, or "thick descriptions" (Geertz, 1973), connect theoretical and analytical points with specific collaborative activities.

We also examine the processes, stages, and predicament of changing roles for educators and organizations. Interactions with others in widening circles of power is a crucial aspect of human development. As Urie Bronfenbrenner (1979) has noted, "the developing person, upon entering into new settings, participates in new roles, activities and patterns of interrelationship." Thus, "activity is at once the source, the process, and the outcome of development" (pp. 288, 287). At the same time, one understands an organization only by trying to change it. Detailed descriptions of collaborative projects provide a framework for understanding complex institutional dynamics.

AN AGREEMENT ON STAFF DEVELOPMENT

Roosevelt is a small district serving 3,200 students, 98 percent of whom are Black. In the 1970s, it had experienced a rapid shift of population and then severe financial stringencies. In comparison with neighboring districts in Nassau County, Roosevelt had a lower tax base and lower achievement test scores. The superintendent, school board, nearly all administrators, and many teachers wanted better schools. That support for high quality education, as well as opportunities for professional growth and personal renewal, fundamentally motivated this collaboration. With a primary school, three elementary schools, and one junior-senior high school, a strong Chapter I program with active parental involvement, and support from Superintendent Ulysses Byas, the resources available were scarcely measured by the contract's bottom line.

Because the contract (initially signed July 28, 1982) allowed a range of possible courses and other activities without specifying who would be involved, Roosevelt attached an expression of its beliefs about continuing professional growth for its staff:

The Roosevelt School District is committed to providing quality education to help students achieve high levels of personal fulfillment, while enabling them to assume productive and meaningful places in society.... We believe that a well conceived and organized staff development program, which is relevant, need-oriented and solution-seeking, will play a significant role in helping students reach achievement levels commensurate with their ability.

After extensive discussions, Roosevelt's leaders anticipated a challenging program:

[It] will provide systematic and coordinated means of involving the professional employees in activities and study to identify inhibitors to wholesome learning, increase expectations, improve supervision/teaching/evaluations, define objectives, and locate resources both within and without the district.

Program developers believed that high teacher expectations encouraged achievement, that supervision could build collegial support, and that persistent, pervasive and powerful patterns of White racism and class bias in America's culture negatively affected Roosevelt's students. School improvement efforts and curricular reforms aimed for the highest quality experiences while guarding against a temptation to blame the victims or to attribute slow progress to some characteristics of students and their families in low-income and minority communities.

For School of Education faculty associated with staff development, the project offered opportunities for systemwide applications of lessons learned from earlier partnerships with Boston and Worcester schools. Certain agendas would have priority in Roosevelt: positive interactions with teachers and administrators who believed in a "hope factor" for children trapped in poverty, who could articulate high academic goals for minority children, and who could fight effectively against the insidious oppression of racism in American society (Gentry et al., 1972). Those agendas were consistent with the mission of the school since the 1970s when positive leadership from Dean Dwight Allen had built a nationally recognized center for humanistic education, innovations, and urban education (Peelle, 1975, 1977).

Faculty described staff development as "activities designed to expand competencies of personnel in an organization over time" (Contract Agreement, 1982). Staff development involved four key processes:

1. Creates synergy from professional and organizational developments.
   —mutual benefits for those involved.
   —both institutional direction and personal growth.
2. Fosters adoption and adaptation.
   —emphasis on communications, group processes, connecting diverse groups in new alliances.

3. Values characteristics of successfully changing organizations.

—leadership, goal clarity, high standards and expectations.

4. Commits priority resources to equity needs.

—not to leave anyone out but to recognize a special place for traditionally disenfranchised groups.

Based on preliminary discussions with staff from Roosevelt and their previous experiences with collaborative staff development projects, Professors Byrd L. Jones and Atron A. Gentry proposed that courses to meet the district's goals would aim

to facilitate comprehensive planning for improved student achievement through the following activities:

—assessments of student needs.

—assessments of parent/community needs.

—projections of educational demands and fiscal support.

—identification of existing strengths among staff and programs.

—examination of characteristics of effective schools.

—review of successful staff development projects.

—laundry lists of promising innovations.

—exploratory or pilot projects to meet short-term needs and demonstrate change strategies.

—collection and dissemination of appropriate products, processes and practices.

—setting priorities and outlining steps toward implementation within an agreed on time frame.

The Roosevelt contract was vague or meaningless—subject to contradictory multiple realities—till participants completed courses and applied change strategies based on these general principles. With comprehensive goals related to ill-structured issues of academic achievement, actual outcomes depended considerably on collegial and supervisory cooperation and on future support and guidance from the superintendent's office and the board of education. Needs assessments and pilot projects required approval by appropriate supervisors; and extensive projects might be stymied by one's colleagues, by principals, by curriculum coordinators, by central administrators, or by a lack of funds.

Staff and parents as well as community leaders needed to be informed in ways that supported their perceptions of their schools' strengths and weaknesses. Improving building climate and classroom curriculum required tacit acquiescence and often active cooperation from many parties in the district. Without these steps and new behaviors among teachers, gains in student achievements were unlikely, nor could positive effects be attributed to the Roosevelt/University of Massachusetts Staff Development Project.

PREHISTORY

A partnership scarcely begins with a formal contract that specifies objectives and activities; however, that agreement between two institutions for developmental purposes depends on trust among key individuals in both organizations. In addition, a sense of shared hopes for improvements and practical benefits in both institutions through interactions among individuals can foster a sense of common direction. In turn, those responses constitute a "prehistory" (Sarason, 1971) that conveys a sense of normal behaviors, current pressures and conditions, and personal relationships among individuals in organizations.

The Roosevelt collaboration was built on rich interconnections that gave plausibility to the words expressed by both parties in the initial contract. Over a decade earlier, Julius Erving and his coach had gone from Roosevelt to the University of Massachusetts. Long Island residents had driven to Amherst for basketball games, and they might do the same for an academic program. University faculty later involved with Roosevelt had implemented programs in Springfield, Worcester, Boston, Hartford, Brooklyn, and Pasadena (California). They emphasized a formal curriculum of innovative instructional and administrative practices that could overcome the economic, political and social pressures impinging on schools serving low-income and minority students. Informal networks, a track record for delivering on one's commitments, and shared values helped to build interest in a partnership.

Byas served as the project's connecting link and most important advocate. He had established a reputation as an outstanding educational leader in Georgia and Alabama based on his personal charisma and his achievements in difficult jobs. He had earned his doctorate from the School of Education with support from a Rockefeller Fellowship. As described by Hugh Scott (1980), Byas

set for himself a very demanding code of professional standards and integrity. He is not a large man physically, but he has an intellectual capacity and curiosity that produce an extraordinary impression of energy. . . . He discouraged any ceremonial difference that might be accorded to him as superintendent. At times, he can be very blunt with friends and foes. Among Black superintendents, he is highly respected and well liked.

Byas conveys a spirit of self-assurance. This self-confidence has been developed from years of successfully confronting demanding responsibilities and difficult circumstances. His colleagues have repeatedly selected him for leadership positions in education at the local, state, and national levels. Byas served for two very important years as the president of the National Alliance of Black

School Superintendents. Few persons can match his skill at producing intellec-
tually stimulating—and witty—statements. (p. 194)

In 1970, Byas was appointed Superintendent in Macon County—an
extremely poor and predominantly Black district in Alabama. He encouraged innovations in curriculum and instruction, built new facilities,
sought external (mainly federal) funding, and raised faculty morale and
student achievement. He encouraged discussions about a joint program
for inservice training and advanced degrees involving Tuskegee Institute
with the University of Massachusetts and Macon County Schools. Before
those negotiations reached a final stage, the school committee changed
membership and no longer supported Byas's commitment to rapid improvements and sound educational practices. Alabama's loss became
Roosevelt's gain.

Roosevelt's schools were in desperate financial straits with low staff
morale when the Board hired Byas. The district had experienced a rapid
transformation from a predominantly White district to one with a 93
percent minority student population in 1977. Surrounding communities
in Nassau County remained almost all White until the 1980s (with the
important exception of Hempstead). An effort to reduce racial isolation
through a reorganization of grade levels known as the Princeton Plan
had instead hastened White flight. Rapid turnover of staff had followed
with five superintendents, six principals at the high school, and a dis-
astrous budget overrun that would be repaid during Byas's tenure.

There were sporadic conversations about a staff development or leadership program; but first the district had to cut costs, reduce its debts,
and lower tax rates while improving educational programs. Eventually,
instruction improved as shown by rankings of student achievement
among Nassau County schools. For six consecutive years, Byas recommended a reduced tax rate for schools in Roosevelt. He made his
presence felt in every building and in most curriculum decisions. He
added microcomputers and technical equipment. He promoted and supported new administrators and encouraged continuity of planning and
instruction. As others recognized his accomplishments and charisma,
he gained a reputation as an educational leader on Long Island and in
New York.

On the university side, there were questions about the feasibility of
a staff development collaboration in another state nearly two hundred
miles away. Like most public institutions, the University of Massachusetts charged substantially higher tuition for out-of-state students than
for residents of the Commonwealth. Also, it imposed student fees that
included health services and support for graduate student activities, few
of which benefited employed educators visiting Amherst one weekend
a month. As it happened, nearby universities on Long Island that offered

advanced degrees in education were private, and their regular tuition was comparable to costs at the University of Massachusetts. At that time, few institutions scheduled courses over weekends to accommodate working professionals.

Extended discussions had preceded contract negotiations, but such informal contacts seldom result in an ongoing programmatic linkage. The Amherst-centered urban education network included a diverse set of professionals: about half were Black, and half were working in public schools. During the 1970s, faculty and graduate assistants had designed and delivered a variety of programs, mostly for preparing new teachers for urban schools. Later these faculty had shifted toward low-cost staff development projects as a pragmatic way to help schools serving minority communities. Those commitments established a basis for discussions and planning till more concrete programs could be supported by Roosevelt and the University.

BEGINNING A PROCESS

In September 1982, educators from Roosevelt began graduate programs at the School of Education. Out of 25 who initially expressed a strong interest, thirteen calmed lingering doubts, paid tuition, and arranged to take care of family responsibilities during four weekends each semester. The stated theme of the first year was simple: "Major organizational changes always require people to modify something about their behaviors." This belief translated into an effort to get participants to work together on positive and practical plans.

Although this approach had a variety of antecedents and powerful support in recent literature about school change (Rogers, 1985), conventional views of research kept intruding on efforts to empower practitioners as experts. University instructors stressed how to make schools fairer for poor and minority students, how to work within complex organizations, how to build teamwork among change agents, and how to foster feelings of hope within a context of social, political and economic realities. Nevertheless, this pattern of action research required careful explanation and "selling" both within the School of Education and among key staff in Roosevelt.

In presenting a framework for research at the opening weekend, Jones (lecture notes, September 1982) suggested that "an examination of American schools in terms of our three criteria—equity, efficiency, and choice—is a shattering experience. Schools are unjust, unfair, and inequitable," reflecting pervasive and persistent discrimination against low-income and minority students. In that context both efficiency and choice become a mockery. Yet, Jones insisted, some poor and minority children have learned in the most miserable classrooms; some teachers have proven effective instructors in buildings with low achievement levels; some urban schools have succeeded with staff and students no different from other Chapter I schools; and some districts have consistently managed to run competent schools despite the competition for funds in urban areas. Thus the well-documented failures of schools to serve poor and minority children are unnecessary. We need case studies to help us understand the successes—not additional explanations of an unnecessary failure.

Gentry and Jones insisted that understanding the effects of racism and class divisions on American society and schools would help in devising change strategies for Roosevelt.

   Their approach responded in part to research that had conveyed a negative tone about urban schools. Devastating critiques of published studies by Cyril Burt and Arthur Jensen (see Lewontin, Rose, and Kamin, 1984) had not overcome widespread beliefs that genetics determined intelligence and that some genotype pools, such as for Black Americans, were inferior. Studies such as the Coleman report could not distinguish current biases from historical patterns of discrimination in determining income and class status. Hence, race appeared as a significant variable for school achievements. When Edmonds (1982) demonstrated flaws in James Coleman's explanatory framework, however, his conclusions about effective schools gained acceptance primarily as support for a back-to-basics movement.

   As participants and professors struggled to understand organizational changes related to improved schools in Roosevelt, they settled on certain themes. According to the Rand study of federally supported innovations (McLaughlin and Marsh, 1978), "successful" programs worked because participants adapted proposed innovations to their particular setting in accordance with their needs and goals. That understanding guided planned activities during the first semester as participants worked together to assess both the strengths of Roosevelt's schools and their needs; to identify what changes might be made; and to implement those new behaviors in ways that fitted Roosevelt's specific conditions, resources, immediate history, and goals, as defined locally as well as through state and federal mandates.

   The first class of the initial semester was crucial for setting a tone and a positive direction. Working as individuals and then in small groups, the class engaged in an exercise in utopian thinking about what makes an ideal teacher and an exemplary school. The group favored teachers who could "communicate effectively regardless of differences," who could "motivate a student . . . by presenting their information in a way that is positive and applicable toward the students' goals," who could "be an important/positive role model for all students," who could "understand that each student learns differently . . . and present curriculum accordingly," and who has "high self-confidence while remaining open to new concepts." Teachers needed energy and enthusiasm combined with an openness to parent and community interests.

This initial activity enabled participants to express their own dreams, to share ideas and beliefs with each other, to learn processes and frameworks for change, and to demonstrate dramatically the richness of ideas and expertise available from other students. The class included three principals, one central office administrator, a reading and a mathematics coordinator at the elementary level, a speech teacher, three special education teachers, and two elementary teachers. In focusing on student achievement gains, this diverse staff generally agreed that useful changes depended on the quality of interactions between teachers and students. They stressed attitudes of openness to children and their families, to new ideas and approaches, to other staff members. They valued a willingness to tackle problems one by one. Overall, they expressed little concern for curriculum methods that preoccupy teacher preparation programs.

Instructors emphasized processes rather than outcomes because usable solutions develop from open communications and agreements about feasibility. Unlike many university-based courses discussing group processes and instructional planning, the goal was to implement specific, needs-related management and curricular changes in Roosevelt's schools that would plausibly improve achievement scores for students. Class members who were principals or central office administrators had to handle delicate "political" issues related to teachers who felt estranged from district decision making or relatively powerless to make changes in their setting. To build functional groups, instructors suggested that senior administrators not serve as leaders, nor should recorders be selected because they could print neatly.

From the start, small groups worked effectively and provided a welcome break from larger group instruction by faculty over long weekends. Faculty circulated from group to group—listening and intervening or commenting afterward in order to facilitate group processes. When some groups felt overwhelmed by negative forces, instructors showed how statements could convey one's views without blaming others. When ideas seemed too grandiose, in light of implicit understandings that few if any additional resources would be available other than schedule adjustments, suggestions were made for pilot projects to test the validity of ideas and to demonstrate their feasibility.

The connections between academic assignments and district strengths and needs could not have been maintained without a Linkage Coordinator in Roosevelt. A district administrator served as a crucial communicator about policies, resources, and problems. Susan Savitt informed other administrators about weekend activities and assignments. She maintained an expanding resource file as well as forms and "official" answers to concerns about assignments or expectations for degree programs. She, together with a part-time secretary and a graduate assistant at the university, eased logistical problems within both organizations. Effective use of time on weekends depended on having materials ready for distribution, advance warnings of concerns and needs, and follow-up between class meetings. As the project continued, other staff filled the role. They facilitated meetings of working groups in Roosevelt that provided mutual support and generated a flow of plans, assessments, and position papers.

With all the uncertainties of the initial semester, one extremely positive resource for Roosevelt manifested itself repeatedly: the staff demonstrated expertise, enthusiasm, and a positive attitude toward the students. White and Black participants worked effectively together, although senior staff in Roosevelt seldom shared their beliefs or dreams. Administrative interventions seemed to focus on problems and short-term objectives—such as preparing for an accreditation visit rather than sharing ideas for the preliminary self-study. In Roosevelt, staff isolation had been compounded by low test scores, publicized financial straits, a bitter teachers' strike in 1972, and reminders of discrimination against Blacks.

NEEDS ASSESSMENTS

During the initial semester, groups designed and carried out systematic needs assessments of Roosevelt residents (including three significant clusters of parents and taxpayers without children), elementary school children (including those attending a parochial school), and students in the junior-senior high school. In addition, a survey of 65 items was constructed and administered to members of the school district's board and key leaders that elicited responses about both existing conditions and an ideal school climate. The assessment teams varied in their sophistication and organization, but all looked at other questionnaires, narrowed the range of issues through preliminary discussions or interviews, and obtained feedback from other groups and instructors about how to obtain the desired information. University faculty insisted that data relate to feasible school improvements and that questions be omitted that aimed to confirm someone's favorite hunch about the frustrations of teaching.

In reviewing the needs assessment results and in visiting the district, faculty facilitators were impressed by the strengths of the leadership, staff, students, plant, and equipment. Residents of Roosevelt, as well as teachers and students, expressed positive attitudes toward their schools. District voters had annually endorsed the school's budget during Byas's tenure. Elementary students liked their teachers, classrooms, and the overall learning environment. Secondary students were supportive of their teachers, most of their instruction, and the school environment in general—although, they complained about such chronic problem areas as disorderly bathrooms and lunchrooms that plague most high schools. Invited to focus on areas that needed improvements, students expressed concern for more structure and guidance in the homework, educational planning, career planning, and better techniques for taking standardized tests.

The board of education and other leaders were quite positive about the district's planning, evaluation, and openness to innovation. Overwhelmingly, those involved in Roosevelt schools felt they were achieving much with minimal resources. They wished others would recognize and appreciate their efforts and support a more positive image of the schools. Typical of Black parents elsewhere, Roosevelt residents had a strong interest in education and its possibilities for children, matched by a sense of frustration that their hopes might not be fulfilled.

The surveys did not directly identify race or racism as problems, but those issues appeared indirectly in comments on achievement, college preparation, single-parent homes, and appropriate steps to build pride in self and schools. Students in the junior-senior high school wanted assemblies to emphasize positive aspects of their school and their culture, and they wanted better preparation for SAT tests. Residents and educators knew that the larger society outside of Roosevelt did not respect its schools. Students need a solid track record for college placements or employment in order to build pride in and respect for their schools and community.

SCHOOL IMPROVEMENT ACTIVITIES

During the second semester, groups re-formed to focus on specific projects or exploratory areas, including use of school plans to foster a positive school climate; parent and community interactions with schools; improved awareness and use of special education programs; teaching basic skills through an integrated arts curriculum; and roles and responsibilities of students in decision making. These projects moved forward both in Roosevelt as activities in schools and on paper as drafts for position papers that would form part of comprehensive examinations for doctoral programs. By general agreement, projects would be approved in Roosevelt by the superintendent (assuming support had been previously obtained from principals and curriculum coordinators) and by the student's faculty advisors.

University faculty believed that viable projects would lead to useful and appropriate dissertations based on a framework of action research.

A substantial part of partnership's budget was used for ordering books and photocopying articles for a resource center located in Roosevelt where participants could share materials and ideas. During trips to Amherst, students engaged in lengthy discussions ranging from "gossip" about work to interpretations of Sarason's *The Culture of the School and the Problem of Change*. The goal was an acceptable project that met Roosevelt needs and priorities, that extended the thinking of both participants and close colleagues, and that involved some risks of failure while also promising school improvement. By acting to change schools, staff could extend their understanding of larger social, political and economic forces as they affected educational opportunities.

Course work had begun with six credits during the initial semester. "Research, Planning and Development for Urban Schools" covered important studies related to class structures and White racism and their impact on school achievements; effective schools and successful staff development efforts; teacher expectations, self-fulfilling prophecies and classroom patterns of time use; and race and intelligence tests in schools. A second course, "Developing Educational Plans for Staff Development," emphasized group work and needs assessment projects in Roosevelt. During the spring semester of 1983, students enrolled in "Urban Administration and School Structures," which covered standard management issues, assigned a textbook, and required a project design with a proposed table of organization and a budget. A course, "Change Strategies for Urban Schools," and its practicum explored the literature of innovations and community development while allowing time for directed readings in specific project areas.

In their third semester, doctoral students who had already earned a sixth-year diploma or had many credits beyond a master's degree initiated work on their school improvement projects and prepared for comprehensive examinations. Taking two courses, they read about organizational development and improving instruction through clinical supervision. In addition, some arranged for independent study in children's literature and reading or other topics. Most participants passed their comprehensive examinations in February and March 1984. Their position papers and oral presentations demonstrated both a sound grounding in their chosen area of school improvement and their own beliefs as educators involved in effective schools serving poor and minority students.

In the fall of 1984, a second group of ten entered their degree work with a similar program of study. This group included five classroom teachers, one central office coordinator, a school psychologist, an elementary school principal, a high school administrative assistant, plus a newly appointed writing coordinator who had taught at the elementary level for sixteen years. Less advanced in their graduate studies than the first group, they anticipated a full second year of course work that would include clinical supervision. Some teachers sought New York State certification as director/supervisor, and they enrolled in a school law course during the summer of 1985. Other classroom teachers focused on curriculum projects, especially reading and writing.

Faculty who offered courses during the weekends visited the district to meet with students individually, to observe classrooms, and to talk with administrators and staff about student projects. They and others offered lectures and workshops for other teachers in the district. Topics included effective schools research and its implications for Roosevelt, children's literature, special education, computers and the future, individualization of instruction, and reading in content areas. In addition, several sessions of supervision cycles were conducted in classrooms to demonstrate how teachers might implement peer observations for instructional improvements.

After the project's third year, most activities depended on the energies and skills of program participants in Roosevelt. As of the summer of 1987, four projects had formed the basis for Ed.D. dissertations, others were nearing completion. A district administrator had enhanced teacher interactions with parents in an elementary school; another had increased use of computer laboratories; and a third sought better readiness for school through instructional responses to early identification of needs at the prekindergergarten site. A veteran principal (the first Black teacher in Roosevelt) had documented his experiences as an educational leader dealing with issues of racism and poverty; another principal involved teachers, parents and students with planned changes related to an improved climate in the high school; and a third provided additional support and training for students in grades four and five who were at risk academically.

Other school improvements included writing, arts, and body movement in the elementary curriculum; reducing math anxiety among elementary teachers; and augmenting resources for teachers of language arts and reading at every level. In light of achievement test scores that were above average through grade six and then fell off, several teachers researched early adolescence and a better transition to junior high school. Positive responses to these efforts have demonstrated to staff in Roosevelt that the district has the expertise and the capacity to implement school improvement activities.

PROBLEMS AND POTENTIALS

There are cogent reasons for school systems and universities to work together on staff development. Slow growth, declining public support, and restricted budgets that began in the 1970s continue to affect educational policies. Cooperation with higher education offers a way for schools to compensate for reduced resources. Roosevelt had justified the initial contract as a response to "the highly emphasized 'knowledge explosion' and its effect on teaching methodologies and techniques, computers and their effect on people, changing culture and its implication for curriculum, decreasing enrollments, the low turnover of faculty, the increase of our knowledge of pupils and the learning process." Inservice education was consistent with a presumption that universities should disseminate new knowledge to adult learners as well as to students. But traditional relationships did not actively involve teachers in their own plans for new behaviors and resources to improve schools.

Institutions of higher education appear to be natural partners for schools, especially for ongoing staff development that builds on the clinical skills of teachers. Despite a general distrust by school people of academic elitism and a university-level disdain for a lack of research and theory among elementary and secondary staffs, the ideas of school and university teachers on many educational matters are "remarkably compatible" (De Bevoise, 1986, p. 10). During partnerships, however, differences develop. Enrollments in higher education depend on individual calculations of private costs and benefits—future careers. Public schools have a direct concern for equity and public purposes related to both citizenship and a fair chance to develop individual and social potential. Teachers, districts, and universities focus on activities most in line with their own interests.

After five years the Roosevelt/University of Massachusetts Staff Development Project had become a collaboration with an identity and accepted patterns of activity. With multiple perspectives, participants looked afresh at their own roles and purposes. Not all those lessons were positive. Systemic barriers to school improvement and broad socioeconomic forces continued to impede educational opportunities for Black Americans. Both formal and informal interviews revealed that Roosevelt staff believed that the program had significantly affected the district. Although achievement test scores in Roosevelt had risen, and the district was no longer in the cellar position among Nassau County schools, those gains could not be attributed solely to the project. But the enthusiasm and leadership of the twenty-plus individuals who participated in course work and remained in the district should sustain positive development.

Educators typically seek appropriate and practical applications that will produce quick results. Many teachers and administrators in Roosevelt expressed their goal of translating theory, research, and professional reading into better instructional practices and/or better climates in more classrooms. This transformation is an unfinished agenda of every staff development project because ideas have to gain support from teachers and administrators, as well as parents and community members, within a common time frame. Once Roosevelt teachers and administrators advanced their own projects, then empowerment built momentum for greater changes. By recognizing their colleagues' skills, teachers experienced more staff working together, students learning despite poverty and racism, and synergistic effects of small projects on the district.

Underlying many comments from Roosevelt participants were reminders of the importance of involvement in processes organized to improve specific facets of the school. Members shared their proposed project ideas with selected friends as a way of learning how their sensitivity to negative feedback cut off comments from different perspectives. A principal included small-group brainstorming sessions as part of faculty meetings in order to elicit ideas on specific issues such as lunch room decorum. This emphasis on process, however, raised questions for those accustomed to conventional inquiry into project outcomes. Under pressure to demonstrate measurable results, staff developers often push a specific pedagogical or management technique rather than ongoing processes of professional development.

Roosevelt staff recognized a need—fully shared by faculty at the School of Education—that program efforts should extend beyond those involved in degree programs. Yet project-sponsored workshops taking place after a school day have little impact on staff behaviors. Ideally, follow-up visits would encourage teachers to try relevant ideas in their classrooms and then to report on their successes and problems. Greater involvement, of course, raises a resource issue because larger numbers increased costs for presenters and staff time. Cost-effective staff development utilizes motivated teachers and administrators whose energies and talents can be mobilized for an extended period of time through advanced degree programs.

Gradually, teachers recognized that they had knowledge essential to facilitate school improvements. They knew the procedures and curriculum as well as the personalities and political pressures of their specific setting. In turn, university faculty learned that knowledge at the cutting edge of research was less useful than suggestions for imaginative adjustments to bypass impending roadblocks and crises. Outside experts must beware of specific recipes for what to do on Monday morning or of becoming abstractly theoretical. Workshops seldom affect schools when they convey that teachers are inadequate, that a good idea will drive out a bad one, that teachers and administrators have different roles and should not work together on school climate, or that instructional gains will not change organizational behaviors.

That presumption that university faculty were experts had hindered effective collaboration in Worcester as well as in Roosevelt till teachers felt empowered to apply their own clinical expertise. Fortunately, graduate programs in the School of Education have been individually negotiated between students and faculty advisors based on the goals, prior learning, and program of academic study developed by each student. Since special programs offered a limited number of courses (either on-site or on a weekend schedule), negotiations about what to learn occurred within the context of certain key courses that required small groups to work on specific school improvement activities. Those projects provided a focus for teachers' readings, visits to other sites, and firsthand experiences with a planned change effort. Those activities made real the participants' own expertise.

As the project unfolded, the superintendent enhanced the image of Roosevelt's schools. Byas reported on the collaborative efforts at the Long Island Association of Supervision and Curriculum Development (October 1984), at the New York State School Chiefs Conference (January 1985), the American Association of School Administrators (March 1985), and the New York State Superintendents' Association (October 1985). The district published a descriptive booklet of twelve pages and distributed some 2,000 copies at meetings and in response to requests from over 25 school districts. Those outreach efforts gave participants and others a sense that their work was appreciated and meaningful in a larger context of school reform.

Despite signs of success in Roosevelt and support from Dean Mario Fantini and several faculty members, the School of Education did not significantly expand its staff development/school improvement efforts. The university's bureaucratic procedures continued to treat teachers as students rather than as professionals in an organizational context. Many faculty were uncomfortable about direct involvement with agendas of school improvement. They resisted sharing academic authority with practitioners. Only a small number of faculty regularly taught off campus or on weekends. Many unconsciously conveyed their elitism and preference for long-term, theoretical studies. Uncomfortable with their interactions with practitioners, these faculty self-consciously proclaimed the virtues of research, large libraries, and statistical treatments of quasi-experimental data. They displayed an unremittingly critical attitude toward other researchers and reform efforts.

As Byas pointedly commented, partnerships such as the one with Roosevelt may represent a long-term investment in American society—if those students who benefit from better schools later choose careers in education. In light of an increasing proportion of public school enrollments from minority groups (from 35 to 40 percent in the coming decade) with declining minority staff (from 10 to 5 percent), there will be a national shortage of Black and Hispanic teachers and administrators, as well as others prepared to work with minority students, teachers, and parents. That education cannot be based solely on overwhelmingly White and middle class college campuses and it must involve effective schools serving low-income and minority children.

Partnerships are always in the process of redefining themselves through new activities, growing understandings, and fresh issues that appear neither in their prehistory nor initial agreement. Such projects, then, seldom have a tidy ending with a sense that all initial expectations and goals were met. Developments are essential if collaborations are to meet their fundamental purpose of creating a locus of different realities and alternative activities that neither organization could easily incorporate within its basic structure. Ideally, partnerships can foster institutional responses to rapidly changing conditions by serving as a "scouting party" for mature organizations. All parties involved with Roosevelt engaged in, and thereby learned new ways to support, school improvements.

5

Parent Organizations, Businesses, and Human Service Agencies

Many partnerships between schools and outside organizations have started with expectations of additional resources and new ideas—only to stumble through episodes of misunderstanding. In one instance, an intervening lobby between a university department of education and an associated laboratory school served to divide as well as to connect their activities. At the time of the space shuttle's initial flight, university students and faculty had been invited to the lobby where a television monitor would show the landing. Just before touchdown, a first-grade teacher brought twenty students to the nearly deserted lobby. There she encountered a staff member from the education department who requested that her class leave forthwith—lest some principle of university-related use of media equipment by compromised.

At times, outsiders demonstrate confusion about school regularities, and minor contretemps discourage interchanges with educators. A teacher in an urban middle school recalled that she had encouraged students to invite residents involved with community health to her classroom. A parent who served on a local rescue squad agreed to talk about paramedical roles during emergencies. A week later, the school's principal momentarily panicked as an ambulance arrived and paramedics rushed into the building. Such dramatic demonstrations of lifesaving techniques upset the school's normal pattern of instruction.

As schools seek outside partners, they need to understand the varying interests and purposes that influence those organizations. Although a great variety of interactions are possible, characteristic pressures shape the cultural patterns not only of institutions of higher education and schools, but also of parent/community groups, businesses, and human service agencies. Just as outsiders should understand teachers' complex roles and the elitism of higher education, educators need to appreciate the voluntaristic nature of parent/community groups, the drive for profits of firms, and the bureaucratic nature of human service agencies.

PARENT AND SCHOOL RELATIONSHIPS

According to many opinion polls, parents and teachers generally believe that both would benefit from greater interactions. More than a million parents participate in advisory councils (Davies, 1978, p. 81). Most schools encourage parent-teacher conferences, yet those relationships often frustrate both sides because they hold different purposes. Teachers believe that parents should prepare children for the school day, reinforce the importance of homework, and accept responsibility for socialization skills. Parents seek influence over curriculum, disciplinary procedures, and staff evaluations primarily for their own children.

Schools, parents and community members are "worlds apart"; as Sara Lawrence Lightfoot (1978) observed, "families and schools are engaged in a complementary sociocultural task and yet they find themselves in great conflict with one another" (p. 20). That dissonance follows from common responsibilities as well as obvious differences. Teachers see families as "the other critical institution beyond the school that shaped the world of the child and defined the primary processes of socialization and acculturation" (p. 8). Teachers face conflicting goals. They can consciously ignore family background in order "to establish an exclusive, isolated environment, free from the intrusions of parents (and perhaps free from the potential bias of stereotyping children into fixed social categories)" (p. 9). Or they can allow social status and income to determine their sense of a child's potential—to the detriment of low-income and minority children.

Schools seldom provide opportunities for debating and resolving parent and community conflicts with teachers. "In fact, schools organize public, ritualistic occasions that do not allow for real contact, negotiation, or criticism between parents and teachers. Rather, they are institutionalized ways of establishing boundaries between insiders (teachers) and interlopers (parents) under the guise of polite conversation and mature cooperation." Although some 5 million parents and teachers belong to parent-teacher associations (PTA or PTO), they sponsor "contrived occasions that symbolically reaffirm the idealized parent-school relationship" (Lightfoot, 1978, pp. 27–28). Activities, such as Know Your School nights, confirm the authority of teachers and school regularities.

In order to affect broad policies, parents and community members have formed voluntary associations to gain information about educational practices, encourage citizen participation on appropriate committees, and influence school leaders. Parent/community organizations have immediate plausibility and high promise as a school improvement strategy, yet they are notably fragile and short-lived. Such organizations focus on broad policies, political forces, and economic resources; but they seldom agree on remedies. Hence, single-cause protest groups often mobilize active opposition to a specific teacher, leader or procedure; but they fracture over replacing the individual or policy.

DEVELOPING PARENT/COMMUNITY INVOLVEMENTS

The problems and potentials of parent/community groups were illuminated by the Greenfield (Massachusetts) Secondary Schools Project. In 1977, Greenfield's leaders convened teachers, administrators, students, parents, and outside consultants in order to individualize academic programs for all secondary students. In keeping with federal mandates under P.L. 94–142, Greenfield planners envisioned a procedure to involve parents with teachers and others in developing individualized education plans (IEPs) for 1,100 junior and senior high school students.

Incorporating research findings about promising ways to promote educational changes, the project proposal insisted on local control to assure ownership of the project by Greenfield people. Project governance called for shared decision-making processes and established separate advisory committees representing parents, teachers, and students. Outside experts were limited to providing advice and assistance. A full-time project coordinator would facilitate communication and cooperative planning. Seed money would support specific improvements in schools.

Despite these ingredients, the project never resolved a series of initial problems that included disputes among committee members over a time line for needs assessment surveys, questions about the coordinator's authority, and declining interest on the part of two key administrators in the school system. As a result, commitment to the project dissolved. Within a year, few parents or community members attended committee meetings. Some parents distrusted program goals; others found elaborate decision making through committees unconnected to their everyday concerns as parents and citizens; still others were uncomfortable about determining educational policies. During that first year, Greenfield participants never identified an activity with mutual payoffs that might have enabled the committees to bridge some of their differences.

With the goal of universal IEPs having foundered amid clashing interests and interpretations of special needs, the project hired a new coordinator, Robert Maloy, in 1979. Seeking a new focus, he emphasized inservice workshops for teachers and grant-writing assistance for the school department rather than organizational self-study and interlocking committees. Additionally, a grant from the Western Massachusetts

CETA (Comprehensive Employment Training Act) consortium provided over $200,000 for a work-experience program that would employ youths who had left school in constructing wooden playgrounds and other recreational equipment for Greenfield's schools.

Parents, community members, teachers, administrators, and high school students came together to design and build slides, sandboxes, jungle gyms, and other climbing structures. Initially, they faced some crucial decisions: Should individual schools design their own equipment and layout? Would the same facility serve both girls and boys? What were acceptable playground safety standards? Would young children use toys that could be built from leftover materials? These questions empowered participants as "experts" on issues of human development and community standards.

Community participation engendered joint decision making. Several teachers assembled curriculum lessons about the construction process for children and parents to share. Linkages were established between juvenile justice agencies and area businesses (especially those supplying materials for the project). Constructing a playground at a summer camp for handicapped children heightened awareness among adults and students about how special needs children learn and play. After CETA funding was withdrawn in 1981, parents worked with teachers and community people on three other playgrounds. A sense of ownership had come more from hammers, nails, and donations of recycled materials than from elaborate committee structures.

Over this period, a School Volunteers Program attracted support, and its members initiated other cooperative efforts. Some parents moved from playground builders to classroom volunteers, and then they became critics of science lessons. They worked with the school system, an environmental education center, and the Massachusetts Council on the Arts and Humanities to help select a new science textbook series. Given mutual support and trust generated through these collaborative interactions, teachers shared meaningful decision-making roles with parents. As often happens with school improvement partnerships, the unanticipated outcomes of the project were at least as important as the planned changes.

PARENT COUNCILS AND SHARED POWER

Parent/school partnerships require mutual respect and a willingness to address complex issues of learning for future societies. Most successful community or parent collaborations flourish in districts with ample resources and a college preparatory curriculum. Poor and minority parents, who often have immediate interests in school reform, lack time and power to influence teachers. "When we perceive the origins of conflict as being rooted in inequality, ethnocentrism, or racism, then the message being transmitted to the excluded and powerless group (both parents and children) is denigrating and abusive" (Lightfoot, 1978, p. 41). Historical failures to address minority concerns have left schools isolated from those parents from whom they have most to learn.

Schools undertake a broad array of social purposes, such as overcoming barriers of previous discrimination against race, gender and special needs; and they offer crucial developmental support to children—especially from those families with two wage earners, a single parent, or health problems. While special programs may serve socially useful goals, "the negative and paternalistic messages are also communicated when schools begin to take on the total range of familial functions—not just the responsibilities for intellectual and social learning adaptive to a changing society but also the dimensions of primary socialization usually found within the family domain" (Lightfoot, 1978, p. 42).

Because schools and families share responsibility for children's learning and development, they must negotiate a truce over roles. Those negotiations often generate conflict when race and class differences are pronounced. "But," Lightfoot (1978) added, "the differentiated roles served by parents and teachers, the alternative environments that are established in which children can discover different parts of themselves, are only workable and productive as parallel and intersecting systems if the institutions have balanced and equalized authority and if there is a shared sense of values, culture, and goals among the adult participants." Unfortunately, too many teachers have viewed low-income and minority groups as powerless and cultureless, somehow "uncivilized" (pp. 187–88).

Parent advisory councils (PACs) hold great potential for promoting sustained interorganizational cooperation between parent/community groups and schools. Many PACs have been mandated by federal programs such as Chapter I, Head Start, and Follow Through or by local districts implementing improvement plans. Other advisory groups have emerged informally in neighborhoods where a single-issue protest group evolved into a community support organization. In other instances, organizations such as Parents Against Drunk Driving have at least prompted discussion of controversial issues.

Substantial evidence supports a conclusion that schools with active involvement by parents are marked by higher morale and better climate (Henderson, 1981). A variety of districts and states have mandated that school planning involve advisory councils. In Massachusetts, this effort included providing funds for innovative projects to school improvement councils composed of a principal, three teachers, and three parents (secondary school councils also include students). California's response to financial inequities ruled on in *Serrano v. Priest* (1971) led to increases in state funding to local school councils that decided on expenditures for aides, new texts, and more teachers.

Generally, parent advisory bodies have had limited mandates: to approve proposals, to be represented in various personnel actions, and to offer advice. Nevertheless, they have served as valuable sources of input for low-income and minority parents whose views differ markedly from many teachers and administrators. Parent Advisory Councils have not automatically raised student achievement, reduced discipline problems, nor raised community support, but they have fostered useful dialogue—sometimes exacerbating tensions and sometimes uncovering areas of agreement.

Voluntary parent and community organizations require careful nurturing by school leaders. They can initiate interchanges of perspectives and generate helpful advice. PACs function best when limited to neighborhoods, a single school, or a feeder system and when they are sustained over several years. Occasionally they generate conflicts and questions that schools have been reluctant to address. On balance, however, parents and community members both respect educators for their knowledge and communication skills and support traditional views about discipline and homework.

PACs reflected a powerful parent interest in better schools, but they were also creations of outside mandates. When laws or enforcement procedures weakened, few PACs were voluntarily continued. As Marilyn Gittell (1980) has noted: "Citizen organizations have little influence on the educational decision-making process. In lower-income communities there is a lack of political action-directed organizations, coupled with frustration over or disinterest in school issues." Bureaucratic systems, especially in large cities, discourage involvement by ordinary citizens. "Citizen access is generally limited; it is especially closed to those who actively seek a redistribution of resources throughout the system" (p. 241).

This issue is not peculiar to schools but reflects a general condition of pluralist democracy in the American political system. Community groups have acted forcefully in angry opposition; but they are poorly equipped to wage bureaucratic struggles with professional administrators. Without anger to sustain them or nurturing support from educators, PACs usually acquiesce. Some parents find jobs as paraprofessionals; more middle-class members take on leadership roles; the system concedes on relatively unimportant issues while satisfying federal guidelines. Because PACs and advocacy groups are most needed where income and status differences sharply divide schools and neighborhoods, the issue becomes one of power: first, in shaping the issues, and then to obtain agreement on one's desired position.

POSSIBILITIES FOR PARENT/COMMUNITY GROUPS

Parent and community groups are easily organized where differences are small, prior commitments are limited, and new plans can include extras rather than basic skills. Cooperation is facilitated when school staff and leadership can communicate clearly and forthrightly their intent and achievements, believe each school is fairly supported by district allocations of staff and resources, and are committed to meeting children's needs. Then parent/community organizations may discuss sharing a broader network of services related to community development in direct and practical ways.

Teachers have to recognize that organized parent participation is often transitory with a high turnover of leaders and members. Although they have high personal interest, parents seldom obtain direct payoff from school betterment groups. At the same time, such groups may be more student-centered—and less involved in politics and personnel decisions—than elected school committees. Because both large urban districts and the county systems that prevail in most Southern states involve broad constituencies and major political and economic decisions, school boards cannot effectively communicate an individual school's strengths and weaknesses. Likewise, they cannot adequately represent the viewpoints of minorities.

When parent councils and community organizations develop over time, educators gradually convey a realistic view of their situations to outsiders, as happened in Greenfield. When teachers hear local feelings and respond openly either by support or a thoughtful counterproposal, they can expand areas of consensus about purposes and instructional techniques. In Greenfield, parents' support for playgrounds and science texts gave those projects an important political impetus.

The potentials of parent/community organizations are realized primarily in communication and cooperation rather than controversy and competition. Local leadership can thereby encourage input from parent or community groups rather than establishing a pro forma appearance of collaboration through "paper" committees. Effective decision making usually depends on informal channels of communication. For instance, parents inform a school principal about the racist behaviors of a teacher and the principal later passes the word that the teacher's contract will not be renewed.

Viewing schools in the context of various public services reveals a host of scarcely recognized potential partners among other community groups. Sometimes schools can collaborate with boards and volunteer groups that are already involved with libraries, museums, theater companies, cable television, recreational leagues, music groups, historical

societies, volunteer emergency medical teams, and church or civil organizations. In addition, schools may link with informal educational
clubs for children and youth such as scouts, 4–H, or Alateens. Because
such participatory bodies often compete with schools for community
support and volunteers, possible partnerships raise immediate issues of
resources and responsibilities that can be resolved only by enlarging the
meaning of education.

BUSINESSES ADOPT SCHOOLS

During a round-table discussion of school reform, educators bolstered
their arguments by referring to apparent needs of local businesses for
skilled employees. They voiced concern that many high school graduates
lacked the basic skills to secure or to succeed in entry-level jobs; and
they recommended imposing minimum competency tests, raising graduation requirements, and improving vocational training. Someone then
cited a recent national survey of employer needs that had concluded
"specific occupational skills are less crucial for entry-level employment
than a generally high level of literacy, responsible attitudes toward work,
the ability to communicate well, and the ability to continue to learn"
(Committee for Economic Development, 1985, p. 17). The educators
were surprised about those requirements and perplexed about how to
train for them.

After more than two decades of little involvement, American businesses have "rediscovered" the public schools. From 1900 to 1950, "almost all school board members were business or professional men, and
public school management was modeled on business management."
Also, rapidly expanding vocational and comprehensive secondary
schools had aimed at "the preparation of students for a productive work-
life." During the 1960s and 1970s, however, the increased presence of
parent and community groups, teacher unions, federal and state officials, and the courts had eclipsed the influence of business leaders. They
came to believe that schools fail "because of unruly students, unwork-
able innovations, militant and uncooperative teachers, and ineffectual
administrators" (Timpane, 1984, p. 389).

Currently, businesses spend over $100 billion annually on employee
training programs, and corporations seek cost-effective ways to train
productive workers. By helping to improve public schools, business can
transfer some of their training costs to the public—especially for general
skills and a readiness to accept responsibility. Also, firms want schools
to develop productive citizens who can "contribute to business as workers, consumers, and supporters of a democratic free enterprise system"
(Barton, 1983, p. 60). Seeking to attract and retain skilled employees,

local companies "see their business interests dependent on a vital community with a good school system at its heart" (Wise, 1981, p. 70).

Business partnerships with schools are complex enterprises because their overlapping interests depend on their context, time frames, economic outlook, and prospects for growth. Most corporate involvements with schools have been brief and episodic, often consisting of a public relations gift or sponsorship of a special event (Mann, 1984). Many large and medium-sized corporations feel no compelling reason to support schools beyond their tax dollars. Some businesses have fostered career awareness programs in local schools as a way to attract prospective job applicants. Others have lent key managers to help schools establish modern accounting procedures. A few school-business projects have focused on classroom teaching or school climate, but most have simply donated funds or materials.

Interactive collaborations between schools and the private sector such as "adopt-a-school" programs offer an alternative to business and professional domination of school committees (American Council of Life Insurance, 1983; Phi Delta Kappa, 1985). In a postindustrial economy, many workers respond to information and interpersonal relations on their own initiative and they must work effectively in groups without direct supervision. Schools do more than prepare students with job skills and most businesses recognize the social benefits of a broadly educated citizenry. Furthermore, the social costs of depressed neighborhoods for businesses and professionals are staggering in terms of public welfare services, community disamenities, and loss of potential markets.

Adopt-a-school programs stress voluntarily developed and sustained connections between individual businesses or subsidiaries and schools. A school district coordinator links firms with individual schools and identifies members of both organizations who are interested in working together. Initially, business partners are encouraged to provide direct assistance, such as volunteers or tutors to their "adopted" school. Once a working relationship has been established, funds or materials may be provided for curriculum or other projects. Such encouragement has produced impressive results—41 school adoptions in Oakland, a nonprofit network for school partnerships in Atlanta, business connections with 29 junior and senior high schools in New Orleans, programs involving all 171 Dallas public schools, and 95 partnerships in Memphis (Phi Delta Kappa, 1985, pp. 89–97). Ideally, adoptions last as long as they are comfortable, productive and mutually beneficial for both organizations.

Starting in 1974, Boston's English High School with approximately 2,400 students, over 95 percent of whom were Black, began an association with the John Hancock Life Insurance Company to support a magnet program emphasizing educational alternatives. According to John Hancock's brochure: "Most high school students delay their search for a career until after graduation. Often this is because they are unfamiliar with what the business world has to offer. As a result many students end up searching for a career by trial and error." Not every student would choose John Hancock insurance, but "a realistic view of the world of careers is as much a part of education as preparation in mathematics, history and English" (quoted in Peterkin, 1981, pp. 117–18).

Robert Peterkin (1981), Headmaster of English High at the time, noted that representatives from both institutions resolved to interact honestly and openly. First, John Hancock officials explored how the firm could best assist in upgrading existing programs and developing new ones. As a matter of policy, they would not negotiate to provide either numerous job placements for students or large expenditures of funds. The school asked for substantive involvement by John Hancock staff. Teachers and administrators told the firm's representatives that "students must profit from enhanced educational programs made possible . . . by actual experience in the market place or by studying business related curriculum" (p. 120). School administrators believed the collaboration would fail if it were viewed by teachers as primarily a public relations gesture.

Following these discussions, John Hancock supported a number of school improvement efforts at English High School. In 1977, for example, Hancock employees helped revise the business department curriculum; conducted employment, insurance, and journalism workshops for students; printed school documents; provided electronic data processing; and made available information about nontraditional careers for women, internship for restaurant or executive training, work-study experiences, and scholarship programs. The Urban Studies Center, English High's city-as-classroom program, drew on the firm's media, law, public relations, and education departments. The school's Medical Alternative for Students in Hospitals Program worked with the company's in-house medical staff. Also, John Hancock funded a graduate course for teachers concerned with low reading scores among students.

School and company personnel learned that effective collaboration yielded unanticipated benefits. Company personnel helped administrators design a computerized course schedule and print a catalog that enabled students to choose their teachers during an open scheduling period. As Boyer (1983, p. 278) observed, "Services that many industries take for granted, such as printing, can be major stumbling blocks for overburdened school systems. Such services can be provided to schools at minimal expense to business, and with a maximal benefit to the school." Able to make multiple copies of new materials, teachers enriched and revised their courses. John Hancock's relatively small annual commitment of approximately $25,000 combined with volunteered time and service yielded a rich range of joint school improvement initiatives

(Peterkin, 1981, p. 141). That partnership has flourished for more than a decade.

BUSINESS PARTNERSHIP POTENTIALS

Collaborative arrangements between particular schools and businesses depend on a variety of local community factors and pressures. For example, many firms—especially mature ones with roots in a community— have periodically underutilized facilities and staff. Taxes can be reduced by voluntary support for school activities. Contributions by business associations, such as a Chamber of Commerce, build community pride through donations of band uniforms or scholarships. Recognizing that some contemporary youth have no responsibilities outside of school while others must accept adult commitments at an early age, many companies have cooperated with schools on work-experience programs or career education activities. Too often, however, high school students in cooperative education programs serve as low-cost, part-time help for stores and fast-food restaurants.

School-business collaborations may experience problems when those involved assume that the partnership should remediate perceived school failures. In this view, corporations compensate for the inability of schools to teach basic skills, "real-world" perspectives, or basic concepts of economics and enterprise to secondary students by contributing to meet school "deficiencies." In return, they get greater vocational awareness (Wise, 1981). Effective collaborations yield unexpected developments such as open scheduling or a corporate volunteer who directed a student jazz quartet. Teachers become less isolated and students gain access to other instructional modes and settings.

Like schools, corporations are marked by a climate or characteristic spirit that may enhance or confound collaborations. Businesses aim to make money for their owners. When they do so by offering a better product to potential consumers at a satisfactory price, they are relatively free to decide what they want to do with their earnings. Because businesses typically have a clear hierarchy and a quick response pattern, executives decide, authorize, and then expect results. By contrast, public schools—whether they are successful or unsuccessful—are held to bureaucratic standards. Educators face certification requirements, state mandates, restrictive rules, unclear hierarchies, little discretion over funds, complex tasks, and high isolation. Concluding that schools are indecisive, businesses may decline to cooperate.

Different firms have developed distinctive "cultures." Deal and Kennedy (1982, pp. 107–23) described four generic organizational styles: (1) a "tough-guy, macho culture" where individuals regularly take high risks and get quick feedback on their actions; (2) a "work hard/play hard culture" that encourages a high level of relatively low-risk activities; (3) a "bet-your-company culture" where big-stakes decisions take many years to play out; and (4) a "process culture" involving bureaucratic procedures and unclear outcomes. Within any corporation all styles exist: "Marketing departments are tough-guy cultures. Sales and manufacturing departments work hard and play hard. Research and development is a world of high risk and slow feedback." Accounting, Deal and Kennedy noted, "sits squarely in the upper reaches of bureaucratic life" (p. 108). Usually one or another unit establishes a dominant tone for a firm.

Hence, educators must deal with a range of potential perspectives among companies as well as within a single corporation. Interestingly, firms that remain locked into one dominant culture make poor partners for schools. Openness to new ideas and approaches allows outsiders to recognize school problems more readily. Moreover, when business leaders understand how the organizational climate of schools affects teachers, they may better appreciate varied styles within their own firm. Because businesses find happier employees when their interests and style match the job's prevailing culture, on-the-job training involves more than literacy and computational skills. Workers who can assess organizational strategies and structures can adapt to changing conditions.

LINKAGES WITH HUMAN SERVICE AGENCIES

Currently, most school districts cooperate with individual professionals in social services, mental health, juvenile justice, or other human service agencies. Federal legislation covering handicapped children and adults mandates Individualized Education Plans (IEPs) and, where appropriate, delivery through "interdisciplinary teams." Those teams include a person with a handicap, parents, guardians or family members, school personnel, and representatives from social service agencies. Ideally, interdisciplinary teams offer comprehensive and equitable services that no one professional or single organization can provide.

Cooperation in providing services to individual children is not easy, as research has shown. Weatherley (1979) contended that the education of handicapped students "is being carried out in a way that serves some children better than others and some not at all" (p. 9). Parents, teachers and direct care workers offer much of the information that is used during IEP conferences; but psychologists and other professionals dominate team decision making. Activities commonly thought to belong in legislative cloakrooms—building coalitions, caucusing, lobbying outside the formal meeting, using information selectively, trading rewards and favors, and mobilizing support—characterize deliberations in many teams.

These tactics reinforce continued disparities in the scope and quality of special education programs.

Although mandated interorganizational activities have often generated self-serving responses, when schools and agencies want to work together they powerfully strengthen individual educational programs. Schools and agencies share broad organizational missions—providing specific educational, medical, legal, or social services to individuals (Sweeney, 1978). Teachers and human service agency personnel describe themselves as professionals and practitioners who offer technical and interpersonal services to clients. In so doing, teachers and agency people define theoretical issues in terms of their own work setting and job responsibilities. Neither sees the interconnections and overlapping roles of schools and outside agencies.

Between 1973 and 1981, the Education for Community Service program (ECS) combined a model program for teacher development with school-agency collaboration. Jointly conducted by the Falmouth (Massachusetts) Public Schools and the University of Massachusetts at Amherst, ECS represented an "unusual experiment in teacher education" (Winsser, 1982, p. 2). It replaced a standard academic approach for preparing new teachers with a process approach (Sweeney, 1978).

The overall goal of these activities was to promote "personal and professional explorations in education" while expanding the "concept of 'teacher' to include a variety of human service, nonformal education roles" (Winsser, 1982, p. 78). Additionally, project planners hoped to familiarize teachers with human service agencies and the professional dilemmas faced by agency personnel. Participants included preservice students, teachers, and community-based human service professionals. They combined a yearlong supervised teaching internship at the high school with a yearlong field experience in one or more community human service agencies. They also enrolled in other graduate courses.

Although support and funding for innovative education steadily declined during the 1970s, ECS prepared teachers for eight years. Out of 108 participants, 100 earned a Master of Education degree. They consistently rated their experiences as highly positive and indicated increased personal confidence and effectiveness as educators. As part of their academic program, preservice and inservice teachers worked approximately twelve hours per week in a human service agency including the county jail, child-care center, residential group home, mental health clinic, alcoholism program, alternative school, or other local social service program.

Participants selected community internships that differed significantly from their usual responsibilities. For example, several secondary teachers chose agencies serving young children. Initially, educators were unsure about their new roles or how agency professionals would respond.

This uneasiness forced some to "examine the learning process firsthand, with its anxieties, frustrations, failures, and successes." Their internships reminded teachers of the "difficult experience undergone by their own students" (Winsser, 1982, p. 140). As a result, teachers reexamined roles of helping professionals:

I spent two hours a week with patients, and another several hours writing up what I had done with them, and then another hour-and-a-half every Friday morning with her [the agency supervisor], discussing what I had done and why. It was necessary to talk about where I was coming from, because all the things I said and did fed into the job. She would point out certain things that I was thinking and feeling, and she would point out that I had a little problem in some area, something I was having trouble resolving myself, and said that was why I thought that person was having difficulty. (quoted in Winsser, 1982, pp. 142–43)

ECS also generated new organizational linkages. After an ECS intern tutored inmates at the Barnstable County House of Correction, other cooperative activities emerged, including "informal follow up studies on individuals who had left school," discussions with prisoners about their educational experiences, and "a tour of the facilities for all Program participants" (Sweeney, 1978, pp. 456–57). Inmates addressed the Falmouth students and an education officer at the jail was accepted by the ECS program. Later, the Falmouth high school developed an introductory curriculum on corrections that discussed strategies for managing behavior problems among adolescents.

Teachers interning in human service agencies discovered the rich complexness of nonformal education:

When you send people out into the community doing internships, first of all the community itself is aided by time and energy and ideas. Then you have the relationship of the intern with the people in the community. So they know about it, they're talking about it, and they think about it. You have what the intern brings back to the group from contacts, information, ideas. It's like natural P.R. work because it's out there constantly being disseminated and coming back. It just multiplies. (quoted in Winsser, 1982, p. 141)

Once teachers became engaged with the work of human service agencies, they could describe hundreds of ways to cooperate on community problems.

COMPLEXNESS OF SCHOOL-AGENCY PARTNERSHIPS

Despite the successes of the ECS, most partnerships between schools and human service agencies face several significant barriers. First, people in schools and agencies have not actively sought ways for their organizations to work together. Few professionals have time to initiate and develop linkages between organizations. Typically, outside agencies interact with school administrators on legal issues, social workers on family problems, counselors on psychological adjustment matters, and cooperative education coordinators on part-time job prospects for students. Those positions are viewed as peripheral to the purposes of the school by most teachers.

Second, the size of human service bureaucracies complicate collaborative prospects. Massachusetts, for example, spent approximately $3.2 billion annually on human services during the mid–1980s. Those funds supported separate departments of welfare, social services, mental health, youth, children, public health, environmental affairs, and elder affairs. Few formal procedures, informal practices, or cultural traditions present in bureaucracies support the development of interorganizational cooperation. Large human service systems give rise to a "circle game" of "rules and traditions that isolate one set of workers from another, clients from workers, and administrators from daily reality" (Withorn, 1982, p. 15). Thus, despite overlapping educational missions and a potential for extra resources from multiple agencies, people in schools find it difficult to work with large bureaucracies.

At the same time, teachers can find working with smaller, community-based agencies just as troublesome. Sweeney (1978, p. 458) distinguished among three types of community-based agencies: (1) municipal or private social service agencies that focus on specific problems like delinquency, mental health, alcoholism or drug abuse; (2) nonformal educational agencies like public libraries, the Audubon Society, or the Woods Hole Oceanographic Institute in Falmouth; (3) experimental and self-help agencies such as alternative schools, hot lines, or group homes for juvenile offenders. Community-based agencies lack sufficient staff or resources for their clients needs. If partnerships are defined as opportunities to gain new resources, many agencies conclude they have little to offer schools. Teachers and community agency people may recognize that they often serve the same individuals but lack a common plan.

Third, schools and human service agencies each need to demonstrate positive results. As Lipsky (1980) noted, "street-level bureaucrats often choose (or skim off the top) those who seem most likely to succeed in terms of bureaucratic success criteria" (p. 107). Youth employment counselors, recreation workers, probation officers and school psychologists prefer less troubled youths who will count in one's case load and generate positive outcomes. Such "skimming the cream" causes schools to suspend unruly students and agencies to send difficult clients elsewhere. Once again, services for low-income and minority students are reduced as members of the helping professions reflect broader patterns of discrimination.

Teachers and agency professionals face another significant barrier to collaboration. Public agencies compete with schools for funding from legislative bodies. Both seek mandates to enhance roles where they have strengths. As a result, most partnerships have developed where both schools and agencies are effective or where competition is limited as in the case of school linkages with jails or senior citizen centers. In so doing, much school/agency cooperation has focused on addressing individuals with well-defined problems. Neither schools nor agencies have emphasized supportive networks and learning communities that are staffed by volunteers from both organizations.

Conducting school improvement collaborations means coping with and learning from differences in the personal and institutional patterns of partners. While individual parents, local business leaders, human service personnel, or university faculty often work successfully with teachers, partnerships require interorganizational linkages. School improvement connections work best when outside partners have differentiated organizational structures that are large enough to sustain mutual activities—but not so large as to dominate a school or district. Organizations that have overriding agendas caused by rapid growth or an institutional crisis are unlikely to have time, resources or interest in pursuing collaborations. Large organizations need to identify subunits interested in assisting schools and then to create a substructure that mediates institutional pressures.

Parent/community groups, businesses, and human service agencies have both overlapping concerns about schools and education and quite different personal and organizational agendas. Specific interests and goals of each outside partner should be clearly understood. Parent and community groups, for example, depend on volunteers who may be briefly energized by major campaigns around specific issues. Businesses offer schools equipment and staff services at convenient times, but they are unlikely to allow those exchanges to reduce their profits. Human service agencies that work with school leavers or suspended students often blame schools for not serving alienated youth. Universities offer to share their expertise but are insensitive to the daily routines faced by classroom teachers.

In addition, differing personalities and organizational beliefs as well as real world constraints such as funding, political pressures, and perceived needs can interfere with agreements on collaborative means or goals. Partners must create forums for open discussions, work on particular issues of importance to each, and cope with some distrust and differences. Then collaborative projects can identify mutual tradeoffs and support activities that reveal multiple realities and ill-structured problems in ways that promote new thinking about education and society.

6

Cooperation and Conflict among Partners

Two students engaged in a brief physical altercation in a high school cafeteria. The principal, feeling pressure from parents and community members to have a safe and orderly environment, interpreted the incident as a "fight" and suspended the pair. Recognizing peer group pressures to avoid appearing as "wimps," the youths had shoved each other only enough to save face; and they accepted suspension as a necessary consequence of adult authority and school rules. Interpreting the incident as normal adolescent behavior, a teacher resolved to speak with each student at a later time.

Although the principal, students, and teacher constructed varied meanings of the cafeteria incident, the dynamics of the scene proceeded as though each actor had recited well-rehearsed lines in a shared drama. Participants had played to unseen audiences; the students imagined the potential reactions of their friends, the teacher sought to avoid a scene with the staff cast as disciplinarians, and the principal envisioned possible newspaper headlines. Hence, no actor perceived a need to explain that the initial altercation had been mainly a show that never threatened anyone's safety. The scenario illustrates how differing realities promote seemingly meaningful and consequential actions—without allowing for discussions of differences or a deeper understanding of events.

Schools generate a multiplicity of dramas as they interact with parent/community groups, businesses, human service agencies, or universities. Particular personalities and settings shape those interorganizational interchanges, but institutionally embedded meanings make some scenarios more plausible and common than others. Representatives from schools or outside organizations typically play roles and interpret events based on characteristic pressures and organizational demands. For example, teachers contend that university faculty could not manage a class of sixth-grade students. Likewise, business leaders view schools as indecisive bureaucracies. Such assumptions provide scripts for many interactions; and they, in turn, reinforce stereotypes.

As with the incident in the cafeteria, disputes arise and brief interchanges occur without partners reexamining or altering their presumptions. Sometimes, conflicting points of view subtly disrupt group processes by blocking agreements or shared activities. While differences and disagreements are inherent features of social interactions, multiple perspectives can also generate positive agendas for collaborative endeavors. At critical points in the Roosevelt, Boston, ECS, and Worcester projects, participants recognized the different realities of others and expressed new understandings of their own attitudes toward school improvement.

In phenomenological terms, some partners gained an awareness of diverse personal and organizational agendas, a willingness to function with the messiness of change, and a fresh outlook on their own activities and organizations. As teachers discussed ideas and procedures with outsiders, they recognized their own professional isolation and unblocked alternative resolutions. Active collaborators shared an outsider-insider perspective. They knew what their organization believed but also recognized "a different drummer." People and organizations learned to manage the complex motives, resources, and potentials present within school improvement collaborations.

A PHENOMENOLOGY OF COLLABORATION

A phenomenology of interpersonal relationships may be illuminated through the analogy of a love affair, as presented by sociologist Peter McHugh (1968). While dating, two people believe they are in love and assume their feelings are reciprocated. During daily interactions, lovers do not perceive their relationship as an issue to be discussed or explained. For each, love is a shared and fortunate outcome of their time together. These assumptions remain intact till someone's behavior— perhaps reading a newspaper at breakfast—forces a reassessment. Then, one partner may suspect the relationship was only an infatuation or question the other's sincerity of commitment. The "actors reconnoiter the immediate scene to see if those original agreements, largely presumed, still can be used to define their relationship" (p. 8).

Interactive partnerships bear a resemblance to McHugh's dating metaphor. After some preliminaries, two individuals may decide to go to the movies on Saturday. They then have to agree on what film, which show, whether to divide costs, and when to have refreshments. After they have tested their constructed realities through their agreements or disagreements over reactions to the movie, they must negotiate about whether, when and how to continue the relationship. Organizational interactions may well involve more formal phases of negotiations, but the range of individuals create at least as many possible interpretations and misinterpretations as dating friends trying to read each other's cues.

As schools seek potential partners, there are many attempts, more or less serious in nature, to identify local organizations with an interest in schools. In their roles as consumers, volunteers and neighbors, educators interact with other community members. Teachers arrange class visits to outside organizations such as fire departments, stores or museums. Those visits often stimulate brainstorming about potential advantages from shared resources. But few of those conversations result in specific commitments. Occasionally, however, key individuals from various organizations arrange an interorganizational meeting to negotiate possible exchanges.

Just as two individuals attend a movie without settling their lifetime compatibility, school partners need to identify specific shared activities without endlessly negotiating all their possible agreements and differences. For example, a neighborhood middle school and a community-based human service agency may want to address issues of vandalism, recreation for children, sites for community meetings, drug and substance abuse programs, meals for senior citizens, or staffing and curriculum projects. Before too long, they must settle on a specific project—such as a clinic designed to prevent teenage pregnancy and sexually transmitted diseases.

Once a specific focus is set, the partners must see what each organization can bring to the table and what it must ask for in return. The school might want community support for the potentially controversial clinic while community members seek some assurances that the facility would educate youths and not simply distribute condoms. Schools and outside organizations have to balance their shared interest in better schools and community development with their diverse, though potentially complementary resources and goals. Frequently, as differences are revealed, the initiators and planners overstate the potential benefits of interaction. As they learn more about each other's habits, capacities and quirks, then trust leads to further explorations or mistrust pushes toward dissolution of their relationship.

When schools know what service they need from another organization, they seek to purchase it. Partnerships on the other hand can be untidy and ill-structured, with unanticipated consequences and crises. For instance, a district may contract with a national firm for hot lunches. That choice, however, forecloses opportunities for buying locally from stores or from farmers who then open their doors for school visits and special projects. Similarly, consultants may explain a particular mathematics text series; but if teachers want yet-to-be defined assistance in many curricular areas, then a partnership with a university opens many options.

MOTIVATIONS FOR PARTICIPATION

Collaborative agreements between schools and other organizations imply that some individuals and crucial decision makers foresee benefits in working together. Ordinarily, leaders in both organizations sense a need for changes that lie outside normal patterns and thus seek a different kind of relationship. In order to simplify and focus their negotiations, they make assumptions about the compatibility of organizational goals. In so doing they "(1) *assume* that their concepts are valid descriptions of the world, (2) *assume* other interactants are using the same concepts in the same ways, and (3) practically never bother to check those assumptions" (McHugh, 1968, p. 30).

Although organizational leaders may define areas of agreement, co-operation between individuals is problematic. For instance, a teacher and a representative of a utility firm may work together on teaching about energy conservation but uncover disagreements over the role of nuclear power plants. In these instances, each partner faces "common-sense puzzles" of the following sort: "How can persons who are simultaneously looking at the same world experience, experience and/or describe that world in disparate and contradictory ways" (Pollner, 1974, p. 36). Diverging motivations for participation result in what we label "obliged to," "ought to," and "want to" assumptions.

These motivations describe a predominant attitude present within a school, an outside organization, or a subunit within either institution. "Obliged to" conveys top-down pressure for organizational collaboration, such as court orders, funding conditions, or state policy requirements. "Ought to" prevails where leaders sense their organizations will benefit from partnerships in some as yet undetermined ways. "Want to" describes the responses of those members of organizations who anticipate personal and professional gains from their involvement in proposed joint activities.

The Worcester/University of Massachusetts Staff Development Project illustrated how complex motivations affected a large-scale endeavor. Teacher Corps guidelines required that each project elect a Community Council with a distinct budget, but the council's mission and responsibilities depended on what its members wanted to achieve. Prior to submitting the initial proposal, school sites and major themes for staff development were determined by a combination of federal policies, the interests of school-based leaders, university resources, and the results of previous school improvement efforts. As such, the proposal represented a series of "ought to" suggestions for involving teachers and others in voluntary activities that would benefit participants, organizations, and those neighborhoods served by the project.

Various "obliged to," "ought to," and "want to" motivations produce differing personal and organizational perceptions about reasons for cooperation, multiple negotiating strategies, and various scenarios of cooperative action. Figure 6.1 (derived from Maloy, 1985) depicts nine possible contexts for negotiating cooperative activities between schools and other organizations. When outsiders who "want to" collaborate with insiders who also "want to" work together, mutually beneficial, practical activities are predictable. These partners can overcome potential disruptions and conflicts. By contrast, formal meetings with pro forma outcomes are the typical result of "obliged to/obliged to" contexts.

In other cases, the results depend on how collaborative associations develop—who is available to attend meetings, how much energy leaders can devote to problematic activities, whether organizations identify appropriate projects, and how readily mutual payoffs are recognized. When people and organizations believe they "ought to" work together, they engage in conversations, meetings, and joint efforts that hold a potential for growth or disruption. Outcomes of meetings involving "ought to" motivations are uncertain and contingent. "Ought to/want

| | | Outsiders' Motivations | | |
		Obliged to	Ought to	Want to
Insiders' Motivations	Obliged to	Mandated meetings & pro forma activities	?	Conflicting communication & activities
	Ought to	?	Formal meetings & uncertain outcomes	?
	Want to	Conflicting communication & activities	?	Agreements on shared activities & outcomes

Figure 6.1
Possible Contexts for Negotiation

to" interactions suggest a likelihood that people and organizations can unite around workable projects. "Ought to/obliged to" negotiations are problematic and less often lead to positive programs.

MULTIPLE REALITIES OF PROJECT DEVELOPMENT

The impact of multiple realities in school partnerships can rarely be predicted in advance. In most partnerships, only a few people strongly want to work together or actively oppose cooperation. Even when both organizations have agreed they ought to work together, the involvement of most teachers and outsiders results from informal contacts. In most unsuccessful cases, collaborations lose momentum, not through open conflict, but through an avoidance of controversy while differences deepen. A school superintendent or the head of an outside organization sends a substitute. That designee misses a couple of meetings, no one has much to say, and little gets done between scheduled meetings. Finally the collaboration fades away or is not renewed.

In 1982, the Lawrence (Massachusetts) Public Schools invited the School of Education at Amherst to explore a cooperative inservice program for school staff that would facilitate the system's voluntary school desegregation plan. As in many industrial cities during the 1980s, Lawrence had experienced dramatic demographic changes. Public school enrollment of Hispanic, Black, and Asian children rose from approximately one in four in 1978 to more than one in two by 1983. Only one in twenty teachers were Black or Hispanic. Fewer than five percent spoke languages other than English. Presumably, staff development activities would introduce new practices and role models to a veteran teaching staff.

Officials in Lawrence believed the University of Massachusetts might enhance the credibility of the system's desegregation efforts, in addition to providing technical assistance in the areas of curriculum planning, program development, and community relations. Further, those officials hoped that graduate credits would motivate teachers to participate in staff development activities. University faculty believed that inservice courses and a graduate degree program on-site in Lawrence could generate revenue, high instructional loads, and research and public service opportunities for the School of Education.

Thus Lawrence and Amherst planners saw potential for agreement in the complementarity of resources and needs within a general framework of adult learning for teachers. Important differences, however, emerged in discussions over various delivery systems for programs. Lawrence staff emphasized personal enrichment workshops and a professional development institute which might offer some credit-bearing courses. University faculty thought in terms of well-planned, academic programs leading to advanced degrees. They believed graduate study would sustain ongoing teacher development activities and prepare new leadership for Lawrence. The superintendent urged intensive staff development offerings related to the district's needs.

If those differences had been prioritized so that degree programs and personal enrichment workshops were deemphasized, there might have been a basis for negotiation and compromise. Instead all four options were offered to school system personnel during the Spring 1983 semester. That array included several graduate courses, a pilot professional development institute, and a series of personal enrichment workshops. Less than one in six of the Lawrence staff opted for any of those activities. Gradually, the project became an unstructured conglomerate of minimally shared school and university commitments. Neither teachers nor university personnel could clarify their disagreements over priorities or express their real needs and inadequacies.

In order to establish an interactive exchange of people, ideas and resources, organizations must identify payoffs. Mutual benefits for individuals or subsets of the larger institution depend on matching resources in one organization with identified needs in another. In reality, mutual tradeoffs seldom occur simultaneously or in ways that appear equivalent to potential partners. Teachers may seek individual coaching on instructional techniques while university planners desire large class enrollments that are cost effective. A first step then is to identify those members of an organization who want to participate and who will become the leaders and active members of a collaborative project. Next, planners must devise cooperative activities that last a year or more and allow time for exploration of multiple realities and juxtapositions of ideas that illuminate ill-structured problems.

ORGANIZATIONAL STRUCTURES AND BEHAVIORS

Organizations enable routine or predictable behaviors to continue without a need for continual bargaining; and in so doing, strategies and structures become institutionalized. Employees within an agency or firm work together without repeated clarifications of roles and responsibilities. Over time, many employees associate their particular function with the larger purposes and goals of their organization. In this way, bureaucratic structures enable industrial societies to plan and coordinate the large numbers of activities required to manufacture, distribute and sell complex services and products. Thus, all organizations, including schools, operate in predictable ways with remarkable consistency, thereby frustrating change.

Interactions among individuals can be depicted as "mutual equivalence structures" (Weick, 1979). For instance, a real estate transaction depends on a willing buyer, a potential seller, a bank to carry a mortgage, a lawyer to convey the deed, an inspector to certify the building, and a belief that each service will be available. Conceptually, society might organize complex relationships around mutual equivalence structures. Third-grade teachers, for example, would work directly for taxpayers and parents by accepting students from second grade and offering them instruction for a year. A fourth-grade teacher could then assume responsibility for education—all without the presence of a formal school organization. Most of the time, "a mutual equivalence structure can be built and sustained without people knowing the motives of another person, without people having to share goals, and it is not even necessary that people see the entire structure or know who their partners are" (p. 100).

An organizational structure divides tasks and responsibilities among individuals to achieve a common purpose. Although initial organizers conceptualize an entire structure to implement their strategic goals and comprehend the many parts and relationships, those organizational arrangements allow staff to implement routine strategies without awareness of the parts. A person's performance within the structure depends on the readiness of others to carry out their roles, and over time the meaning of the job is defined by its relationship to the work of others. For instance, the curriculum offered by a ninth-grade English teacher makes sense only in the context of earlier lessons in grammar and spelling, later reading of novels, the variety of disciplines offered, and the work of custodians, textbook publishers, and bus drivers.

Interactions within organizations have some characteristics of bargaining among separate individuals or groups, and some characteristics of lovers. For example, many functions of an elementary school—such as lunch schedules, health examinations, student promotions, parent conferences, and the arrival and departure of buses—all fit together, although they are taken for granted and rarely questioned by those involved. Unlike market transactions where accounts are balanced in agreed on dollars and cents, organizational patterns depend on trust among people that some motives and realities are broadly shared. Most of the time, well-run organizations create an ethos in which members share vocabulary and meanings.

While individuals and organizational subunits share the larger goals, vocabulary and ethos of their setting, they also maintain their own realities. In schools, teachers may want inservice programs with universities while guidance counselors, social workers, and administrators desire better linkages with human service agencies. Within business firms or parent groups, some members have time to work in school programs while others welcome involvement primarily as an opportunity to share information. Any organization has multiple interests and reactions to new circumstances, despite the efforts of leaders to direct activities toward a common institutional mission.

Differences in perspectives further complicate interactive processes. Building and sustaining social interactions within complex organizations require people to have reasonable assurance "(1) that a person's behavior in some circumstances is predictable, and (2) that other behaviors can be predictably related to one's own activities" (Weick, 1979, p. 100). Yet that predictability conflicts with a desire to try new approaches that may enhance organizational effectiveness. School improvement partners often encounter difficulties when familiar signals yield unfamiliar responses. Those conflicts may lead to disruption or may generate discussions that create a sense of cooperative possibilities.

Through discussions and interchanges of a voluntary nature, new purposes, goals and broad understandings evolve as some members of organizations gain perspectives, skills, and a fresh sense of empowerment. Ultimately school improvement requires that policymakers, school leaders, teachers, and their outside partners see new ways to facilitate learning. Then students may construct a social reality that is less hierarchical and more empowering to all individuals. But new behaviors and perceptions seldom follow linearly from a neat pattern of cause, remedy and outcome. No one has a well-structured plan for moving toward a future that is largely unknown.

EQUITY AND DILEMMAS OF NEGOTIATION

If interorganizational cooperation depends primarily on understanding the multiple realities of various individuals, then the role of outside partners is complex, but relatively straightforward. Planners should proceed in an exploratory fashion to test those different perspectives. Needs assessments, regular evaluations, and extensive discussions about goals, roles, means, and procedures would help in this process. Communication skills would prove both necessary and sufficient. But normal organizational interactions discourage any understanding of unfamiliar wants or needs till some vague but immediate crisis threatens the constructed realities of teachers or outsiders.

Individuals engaged in improvement activities have difficulty identifying their weaknesses, vulnerabilities, uncertainties, insecurities, doubts, and fears. As a result, many negotiations resemble interpersonal dynamics associated with the "prisoner's dilemma." That conundrum takes its name from a story about plea bargaining. Two prisoners are separately interrogated and informed that the other has already confessed. If both admit guilt, then each will receive a reduced sentence of one year. If both plead innocent and are later found guilty by a jury, they will receive a sentence of five years each. If Prisoner A pleads guilty in the expectation of a reduced sentence and B pleads innocent, then A is sentenced to eight years and B is released. A payoff matrix is shown in Figure 6.2.

The prisoner's dilemma characterizes many interactions among potential partners. At the outset of joint activities, partners routinely see benefits both in cooperating and in merely pretending to work together. The dilemma emerges when partners are unwilling to acknowledge that they both share responsibility for education's plight. Assuming the other partner will see the logic in cooperatively pleading guilty, each defects in order to avoid any penalty. Thus, when schools identify a specific weakness to encourage offers of support, outside organizations are allowed to donate used equipment or personnel time without cooperating around new educational patterns or relationships. Such short-term exchanges or services leave existing school regularities intact.

As partnerships develop, other opportunities for noncooperation or defection occur. As a negotiating tactic, planners from outside organizations may refuse to consider certain requests. Universities may assign their less popular faculty to inservice courses, or schools may seek assistance for insolvable issues. Yet schools will not change unless they construct new organizational realities through improved capabilities. Similarly, outside partners will offer little more than token support till they recognize their share of responsibility for the failure of schools in American society.

Can cooperation emerge among self-seeking individuals without a central authority or an organizational hierarchy? Whether participants

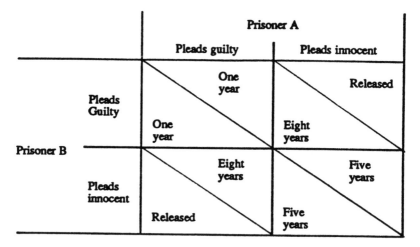

Figure 6.2
A Prisoner's Dilemma

view a cooperative venture as a win-win or a competitive win-lose situation depends on their understanding the possible positions of others, finding mutual payoffs, trusting the good motives of the other partner, and reducing discussions of weaknesses and problems to a manageable level. If modest payoffs and minimal risks are established at the outset of cooperation, then partners are more likely to work together toward some agreed-on goals. Gradually, trust and vocabularies become shared and planning succeeding rounds of activities becomes easier. As Robert Axelrod (1984) has demonstrated, cooperating leads to cooperation and defecting to distrust and disengagement. After many negotiations—or an infinite time horizon—cooperation becomes the preferred strategy.

Alternatively, when partners believe their interactions involve a win-lose outcome, they negotiate cautiously and demonstrate little trust. Assuming she or he must win in order not to lose, a partner demands something the other partner probably cannot grant. For example, teachers demand blanket approval in advance for their new curriculum; schools ask businesses for unrestricted funds or commitments to hire a fixed number of graduates; parents seek veto power over the choice of a new principal; or agencies want the right to place juvenile offenders in schools.

Such reactions are a predictable response to the prisoner's dilemma because they forestall a win-lose negotiation. These preemptive challenges shift the appearance of mistrust to the other party. Thus, they are often used by a weaker status group in addressing a more powerful entity. Typically, outside mandates or funding agencies have sought to restructure local power arrangements by involving disenfranchised groups. Those pressures have induced negotiations but they seldom overcome prevailing mistrusts. Because school improvement necessarily involves some rearrangement of power relationships toward greater equality of rewards, preemptive challenges and hidden agendas regularly confuse collaborative bargaining.

Although leaders in schools and outside organizations would like to reduce barriers to change within their own group, individuals within those organizations often resist. Some prefer to maintain routines or their own status while others look to alter established patterns and power relationships. Useful communication between insiders and outsiders reveals weaknesses and raises questions ordinarily left unaddressed within one's own group. Such revelations may preclude reasonable agreements among potential collaborators. At the same time, those conversations offer great potential for promoting reforms in schools and society.

SCHOOL IMPROVEMENT PROCESSES

Particular organizational and cultural experiences largely shape the theoretical concepts and everyday expressions used by people in thinking about change. When teachers, administrators, children, parents, business managers, university faculty, agency workers, or others are brought together in a partnership, they typically evaluate any changes in light of their position or status within existing hierarchies and their perception of their organization's viability. Teachers want to participate when they see personal and professional advantages in shared activities and when they sense that their partners recognize both their strengths and their problems. But collaborations can accomplish different purposes through common activities, thereby gaining a sense of shared goals that can be reached through diverse means.

Weick (1979) argued that groups may initially cooperate around common means. At the outset of an organizing process, "there is no immediate requirement for a shared goal." Although members have different experiences and goals, "to achieve some of these diverse ends, concerted, interlocked actions are required." Once group members "converge on interlocked behaviors as the means to pursue diverse ends, there occurs a subtle shift away from diverse to common ends. The diverse ends remain, but they become subordinated to an emerging set of shared ends" (pp. 91–92). If a partnership evolves, common means will lead to common ends that will in turn generate diverse means. Eventually, partners may discover that a new set of diverse ends dominates their relationship.

Weick's interpretation of group interactions helps explain why "obliged to," "ought to," and "want to" contexts are important for negotiating school partnerships. In Lawrence, the organizing sequence was cut short. Planners from the school system and the university never found mutually acceptable ways to address such diverse goals as school desegregation, the professional development of teachers, public service by a state university, and personal enrichment of educators. In Boston, Worcester and Roosevelt, however, broadly diverging goals were met by common means such as school improvement teams, community school-site councils, and graduate degree programs for experienced educators.

In Figure 6.3, we present a comprehensive systems model of school improvement that specifies agents (in boxes) and their connections through some typical implementation strategies. Although pressures and influences flow most visibly down the depicted hierarchy, each stage allows for feedback and possible collaborative interactions. Educational policymakers and school administrators allocate resources, set evaluation standards, define curriculum goals, and address equity concerns. In turn, teachers allocate time among students, devise instructional strategies, and create programs and tests to implement those purposes. This framework illustrates the complexity of educational change, and it shows

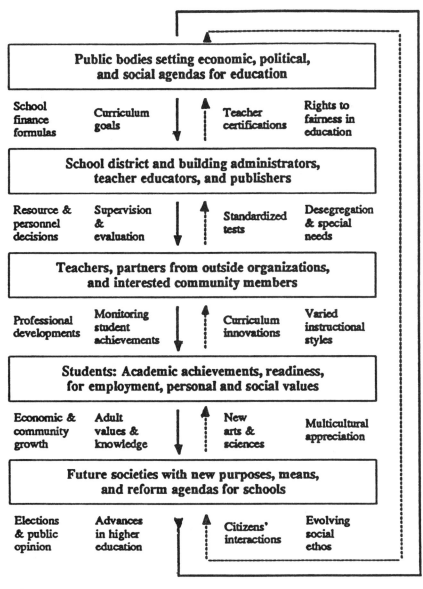

Figure 6.3
A Cycle of School Improvement

why reforms that focus on particular agents or strategies fall short of their desired results.

This cycle suggests how complex motivations (which we have labelled "obliged to," "ought to," and "want to") have affected school improvement collaborations. Community pressures, legislation, and court orders convinced school leaders that they were obliged to pursue partnerships. In turn, many administrators fostered a positive environment in which teachers and members of outside organizations believed that they should develop mutual programs for staff development and innovations. Within that context, those who wanted to build collaborations participated in activities aimed at improved school climate and equitable outcomes for students.

Most school collaborations have started with an impetus from public bodies that reflect larger social concerns for educational reform. Partnerships have been encouraged or discouraged by funding formulas, certification requirements, special programs, school board policies, and attitudes expressed by educational leaders. In particular, interactive collaborations have depended on how districts responded to legislative mandates, political pressures, and community interests. Pluralistic interactions shaped efforts to modify classroom behaviors and those improvements have affected individual and community possibilities for future generations that will lead to new public agendas.

Hence, practical negotiations and stages of program development have begun with positive signals from society and school leaders—or top-down commitment. Ultimately, however, they depended on those who anticipated personal and professional benefits from collectively engaging in school improvement—or bottom-up involvements. Those interactive processes involve many levels of decision making and must be sustained for several years before new behaviors are visibly part of school regularities.

KEY STAGES FOR SCHOOL PARTNERSHIPS

The presence of cooperation and conflict within a broad school improvement model suggests that partnerships develop through a series of stages each with particular potentials and pitfalls. Following embedded scripts, individuals define aspects of their collaboration differently. Over time, those in key positions may find it more difficult to ignore or justify diverging interpretations. Then, seemingly unimportant incidents accentuate doubt and mistrust, and participants struggle to explain why a promising collaboration apparently did not achieve its goals.

In interactive collaborations, an initial sense of trust and commitment helps participants overcome early disagreements. Joint activities generate sufficient mutual benefits so that participants interact informally as well as in planned exchanges of services. A few individuals act as ambassadors or translators, communicating limitations and realities within and between organizations. Those most actively involved renegotiate their relationship with their own institution so that new roles can be accommodated. Eventually, individuals and organizations reveal enough of themselves to generate an internal consistency and integrity to their partnership.

In so doing, partners build shared visions that incorporate differences and modify their existing behaviors. Hence, developing partnerships should not be viewed as a series of specific implementation procedures, but as a periodic emergence of "critical points." Key junctures include (1) identifying the diverse interests of the partners, (2) agreeing on shared activities, (3) implementing joint programs, and (4) planning for future efforts. During those junctures, multiple perspectives and interests play out through possible scenarios that determine whether cooperation or conflict will dominate personal and organizational relationships. Implicit and explicit negotiations build toward dramatic resolutions, and partners must allow the process to be messy but not so confusing as to frustrate progress.

A first critical point revolves around the separate interests and core missions of the partners. They must differ enough to show that each has unique resources that are essential to a shared game plan. Finding and defining that overlap is not likely when institutional survival seems threatened or when all is going well. Thus, cooperation is fostered when organizations and their members have a degree of self-consciousness about their strengths and weaknesses. Often outside support is especially welcome when an organization has a sense of uncertainty about future directions—while recognizing that divergent strategies might augment institutional viability. For instance, when separate groups make legitimate demands on schools, a framework of alternative programs, each linked to outside partners, may meet those demands while allowing the system to "hedge its bets."

An experienced administrator proposed a set of guidelines for initiating partnerships:

1. build initial agreements about problems and their priority;
2. propose some ways for potential participants to start working together;
3. clarify the self-interests as perceived by each organization and key participants;
4. obtain and publicize endorsements from authorities in each organization;
5. build tolerance for open-ended processes, outcomes, and abiguous goals;
6. recognize different constraints and strengths inherent in each organization and its subsystem; and

7. make sure that each side puts something it values on the table so that benefits look probable and defection is not costless. (R. J. Clark, personal communication, May 1986)

A second stage involves arriving at agreement on some common means, usually toward diverse ends, and negotiating safeguards so that each party gains (although not at the others's expense). Even if organizations "put their cards on the table," individual interests are affected in differing and unpredictable ways. Few teachers readily see payoffs in revealing their self-interests. Sometimes longstanding tensions surface as when Black teachers in advanced degree programs are expected to establish a trusting relationship with an all White faculty from a nearby college. Thus, within an organization, some individuals may seek out collaboration while others reluctantly tolerate shared activities, object to their colleagues dual loyalties, or actively sabotage the partnership.

Once negotiations are completed and resources have been obtained, a third critical interchange involves basic issues of staffing, implementation, and administrative follow-through—each of which can be complicated by overcommitments or underfunding. In the abstract, both sides of a partnership may agree on a process for naming a director or liaison, but few individuals meet all the specifications in everyone's mind. Criticism of specific persons or activities is easy and plentiful. Most scheduled meetings conflict with someone's plans. Schools and outside organizations may unload their staffs' "deadwood." When members are divided in their assessments, then collaborative activities become another locus for existing disagreements.

For those collaborative efforts that avoid disruption during stages one, two and three, there remains the conundrum of success. When projects resolve original problems, the new situations typically create different needs. Thus, under the best of circumstances, collaborators look for a graceful way to terminate their partnership before it becomes unwanted or to renegotiate new means toward a new set of diverse ends. When partnership activities win accolades from others, they accentuate charges of divided loyalties among colleagues. Positive evaluations that emphasize partnership goals may alienate organizational leaders who support their distinctive institutional mission. Those leaders want shared activities primarily to accomplish separate rather than mutual goals. Sometimes geographical proximity or established personal relationships create strong pressures to renegotiate formal linkages between organizations.

The presence of critical junctures also suggests a final point about cooperation and conflict among school partners. When partnerships continually renegotiate to reduce or avoid conflict, the partners may foreclose new understandings about what they would like to achieve. In those situations, partners respond to immediate events, but they rarely stop to reconsider their reasons for working together. They engage in complex interactions from unrecognized cross purposes. They "avoid the very situations in which they might learn about them" (Garfinkel, 1967, p. 70). Since superb ideas for the best system will not succeed unless participants understand implementation processes, many partnerships have generated neither interest in, nor trust from, the majority of people involved.

Tensions and disagreements between partners do not have to stymie successful collaboration. Thinking reflexively, individuals can understand how mission, organizational interests, staffing, implementation and evaluation are generated. Only as these activities are completed is it possible for partners to review them and reconstruct meanings. Multiple realities can lead to alternative visions for improving schools. Working within and among self-sustaining partnerships facilitates an understanding of diverse organizational cultures and ill-structured problems. Reflecting on those organizational and personal perspectives can yield new understandings of individuals in a postindustrial society.

PART THREE

EVOLVING UNDERSTANDINGS

7

Collaborative Activities and Teacher Development

An elementary teacher in Roosevelt (New York) applied her background in dance and movement to develop a school improvement project. Years earlier, Ethel Grossman had studied with Martha Graham, Merce Cunningham, and Barbara Clark. During the previous decade, she had experienced the daily confusions of a classroom where young children continually fidgeted, moved around, and were easily distracted. Dance instructors had well-developed techniques for establishing relaxation through breathing and awareness of the body through specific movements and exercises. She adapted some of those exercises for her class of third graders and later for second graders.

Grossman's project log revealed some uncertainties about the "how and why" of this new curriculum—as well as her enthusiasm. Relaxation techniques and quiet exercises calmed the class after lunch or recess, and she noticed the children spoke more softly and avoided banging their desks, books and pencils. She watched Jack LaLanne's physical fitness show on television to learn how to conduct large groups in physical exercises. Later she read Jean Piaget and other scholars to see how they linked physical and cognitive development. She delighted when her students triumphed in small motor control, improved their concentration for achievement tests, and enjoyed exploratory responses such as mirror imaging.

Few teachers have professional training as a dancer, silversmith, chef, carpenter, or nurse practitioner; but most bring an amazing variety of interests and talents to their school that are rarely utilized. Typically, teachers apply their skills in extracurricular activities such as sponsoring a debate team, designing bulletin board displays for corridors, or preparing snacks for special occasions. Grossman had directed acclaimed plays and dance productions, but she had not previously integrated her training into the basic school day. Her diary illuminated a revitalization of her sense of competence, her interest in learning, and her interactions with others.

EMPOWERING TEACHERS

When collaborations foster an educational setting that both empowers individual professionals and supports change, they enhance teacher development. After working for years to improve instructional practices, Bruce Joyce (1981) has envisioned schools where "a vibrant, synergistic environment for professional growth pervades the teaching profession" (p. 128). In such settings, a teacher "has training in supervision and teacher training, studies organizational development, participates in the continuous study of the curriculum areas, has help with children who have special needs, is near a curriculum resource center, and regularly studies new teaching strategies." Professional and organizational development involves both outsiders and insiders. "New ideas for teaching the academic subjects, new technologies, and new ways of working together will come from outside and also be transmitted from school to school as they are developed in the local scene" (pp. 134–35).

Effective school partnerships assume teacher motivation and competence, and they promote growth through open communication and shared projects. In countless collaboratives, teachers have worked in groups on planned activities to enrich their classroom curriculum and their students' achievements. Those teachers have presented themselves to others in new ways, tested different visions of reality, addressed deeper issues of education, and learned about themselves and their setting. Outside partners cannot do those things for teachers; but they can provide challenges to preconceived ideas, an impetus for action, some new resources, and alternative frameworks for viewing schools.

Interactive partnerships provide occasions for teachers to think, talk and act on their beliefs about what would be better for education. Contemporary American society appears highly individualistic and materialistic (Bellah et al., 1985) and school patterns that involve cooperation and social values of equity create conflicts for students and teachers. When schools simplistically rank order individuals through test scores, they ignore the fact that both high achievers and school leavers have to work together to sustain future communities. Teachers have to demonstrate their own enthusiasm and competence, convey a renewed sense of purpose to students and colleagues, and effectively overcome the barriers to change. When improved instruction breaks through the negative social forces imposed on schools serving low-income and minority neighborhoods, staff can take pride in their professional standards.

When collaborative school improvement activities foster settings in which educators feel competent and empowered to meet new challenges, teachers have opportunities to reflect on their professional and bureaucratic dilemmas. In so doing, they understand their daily coping strategies with less ambiguity, obtain support from others, and risk attempting new instructional and managerial approaches. Then teachers will collectively share responsibilities, make decisions, initiate changes, and welcome new partners in school improvement.

STAFF DEVELOPMENT PLANS AND PROCEDURES

In order to empower teachers, activities must affect their instructional and management activities. In her excellent examination of urban schools, Eleanor Leacock (1969) identified a central paradox:

Teachers are the central carriers or perpetuators of school practices that socialize children for future status in accord with the status of their parents—often at the expense of *education* itself—but it does not follow that, as individuals, they are in a position easily to do otherwise. Teachers cannot simply interact with the children in their classrooms, according to their desires and personal style. . . . They must adapt their style, not only to the children, but to the institution, to the principal's requirements, to the other teachers' attitudes, and to the standards according to which they will be evaluated. (p. 202)

In Leacock's view, as the knowledge base expands and instructional materials flood the market, teachers must have time and space to read, discuss and reflect on their practices.

Although universities seem natural contributors to staff development projects, that conclusion ignores the fresh perspectives and additional resources available from other organizations. For example, support from John Hancock enabled the Urban Studies Center to utilize other sites throughout Boston. Likewise, when Susan Savitt (1986) organized workshops for teachers in Roosevelt around ways to work more effectively with parents, she found parent volunteers and other teachers extremely effective in making key points. Community members reconfirmed their apprehensions about teachers and schools. Teachers who had good rapport with parents shared specific experiences and scripts for interacting with adults during difficult situations.

Partnerships to improve schools should incorporate good staff and organizational development practices, although their substantive areas depend on student needs, teacher interests, and district goals. According to Betty Dillon-Peterson (1981), staff development sustains "personal and professional growth for individuals within a respectful, supportive, positive organizational climate having as its ultimate aim better learning for students and continuous, responsible self-renewal for educators and students." Organizational development involves processes "to define and meet changing self-improvement objectives, while making it possible for the individuals in the organization to meet their personal and professional objectives" (p. 3). Activities address specific issues of classroom management, advising, or staffing and scheduling in light of new resources and perspectives introduced by a school's partners.

While many projects may improve schools, certain ideas and proposals are difficult to shape in positive directions. Indeed, teacher-identified needs commonly include many unpromising suggestions. Some involve superficial manifestations of deeper problems—for example, students in corridors and tardiness may reflect poor instruction by inept teachers rather than unruly students or lax discipline codes. Some needs point to absolutely intractable issues—in the sense that they mislabel as a "problem" some facet of the school's core regularities, such as conflicts between individualization and group schedules. Still others identify a panacea or device to relocate the "problem." For instance, acting-out behaviors or low scores on standardized tests are not resolved by assigning kids to a "time out" room or a special needs resource center.

Many proposed innovations presume that more rewards for those already succeeding will motivate others. There is startlingly little evidence for that belief. Programs for talented and gifted are easily corrupted into an elitist setting with extra resources for those who are related to important people, complaining parents, or teachers. Honors programs and open-campus privileges for "A" students are not wrong in themselves, but are tolerable only if other programs and privileges meet needs of others—such as sports, relevant vocational training, school newspapers, student patrols, and so on. If a school supports a variety of programs, nearly all teachers can find a group with compatible styles and learning goals.

Based on the experience of the University of Massachusetts/Worcester Staff Development Project, teachers can work together to promote a positive school climate through (1) outreach to parents, other community members, and community-based institutions; (2) linkages with outside groups such as teacher centers, state agencies, colleges and universities, recycling centers and other sources for low-cost/no-cost materials; (3) a respect for cultural diversity, informed by a sense of the oppressive forces of racism, sexism, and class bias; (4) collaborations with outside organizations to support alternative learning environments; (5) curriculum related to social and economic forces affecting prospects of youth; and (6) use of regular governance procedures (school and departmental staff meetings) as well as ad hoc groups for comprehensive yearlong and long-range planning.

The time and resources budgeted for professional development and organizational improvement efforts should effectively support those activities. Certain behaviors should be rewarded for augmenting resources and empowering teachers. Without assigning roles or designating tasks, a school might reward teachers and others who

1. establish rapport and communicate with parents around steps to improve the school;
2. individualize instruction to meet educational, language and cultural diversity;
3. work well in teams and share successful curricular developments;
4. negotiate to attract new resources and power blocs;
5. respond sensitively to oppressive forces of racism, sexism, classism, and cultural biases;
6. utilize holistic approaches that connect the formal and nonformal curriculum with consistent expectations for all students;
7. recognize their role as models for adult behaviors and peer interactions as well as a source for subject area knowledge;
8. support and encourage others through peer supervision and realistic self-evaluations;
9. discuss how their class and school fit into a framework of community-based education (including the mass media); and
10. support community growth leading to good prospects for a job and a pleasant neighborhood.

Rewards include anything that supports continuing efforts—for example, coffee and fruit for after-school meetings, prompt typing of curriculum proposals, clerical assistance for arranging field trips involving parents, or recognition from building administrators. In discussing incentives and disincentives for change in schools, Sieber (Lehming and Kane, 1981) argued that managers must understand how interventions often threaten "certain fundamental and customary rewards . . . as with role efficiency, task/role autonomy, positive appraisal of pupil effects, and supportive peer relationships." He concluded that the likelihood of success would be greatest when "an incentive system projects an image of a school that is socially integrated, goal-oriented, adaptive to new opportunities, and motivated to contribute to the welfare of clients and the health of the organization" (p. 162).

INITIATING PLANNED CHANGE

Our confidence that collaborative activities promote the growth and development of educators has been strengthened by both personal observation and feedback from practitioners. Also, we have examined outside evaluations of partnerships and many published reports of successful collaborations. We focused on how teachers understood their experiences in school improvement partnerships. Did they feel differently about themselves and their work as the result of their participation? What new attitudes and understandings among school people were revealed in their self-reports?

From 1983 to 1985 we conducted formal and informal interviews with teachers and administrators who participated in the Boston and Roosevelt school improvement partnerships. An interviewer questioned selected educators in order to assess their responses to major partnership goals. Other feedback came from open-ended reactions relating teacher-initiated change efforts to relevant literature and contemporary reform proposals. We observed teachers and teams both in their schools and during university-sponsored classes, and we analyzed reports submitted as part of standard academic requirements.

We summarized the comments of teachers about their experiences in initiating planned changes under six themes: professional revitalization, improved clarity about educational goals, understanding group processes, teacher-initiated applications of professional literature, new perspectives on school cultures, and personal growth and involvement. These characteristics were consistent with outsiders' observations of teams and insiders' summaries of change projects in their schools. They revealed a sense of competence and engagement in contrast to pervasive patterns of conservatism, isolation, and ongoing struggles to cope with classroom dilemmas.

First, project participants reported a sense of revitalization and new professional goals based on their improvement activities. An administrator noted, "I feel less frustrated, more optimistic." Another respondent spoke of "renewed energy" following sessions at the university. Teachers in Boston summarized their positive morale based on working together as "caring among us, for each other, for the school, for kids, for the job." They believed that once a mood conducive to "such feelings has been established by a group—and it does not occur by chance—any task, indeed, can be accomplished."

Second, respondents had connected planned activities to their school's mission. A teacher-administrator noted that his academic work had helped to "get my feet on some solid ground . . . I have an idea where I am headed; there is no wasted time or energy." Others spoke of greater understanding about schools and innovations. A teacher emphasized "the importance of . . . being able to articulate one's philosophy and beliefs." Teachers designed a school climate questionnaire to emphasize feasible projects and strategies for involving students and other staff. An administrator who had aimed to achieve a safe and orderly environment came to see it as a means to student academic achievement and social responsibility.

Most participants linked their optimism to a third major theme—group processes among teachers. Many spoke about the support and empowerment experienced in sharing tasks and ideas. One teacher noted she was "very much impressed with the 'team approach.' The members of my team and I have addressed some very critical issues . . . mutual cooperation and respect for one another's ideas are paramount." Many teachers noted a significant increase in information-sharing among the staff, as well as mutual support in carrying on both professional and academic responsibilities. One reported a shift from being "private and isolated in my work" to valuing group processes. "I see more willingness to share, to trust one another, and to work together in collaborative efforts." Consistently, teachers spoke of becoming more patient and tolerant of others and "more inclined to gather input from other people." Effective groups facilitated "an exchange, which is more substantial, between several schools."

Fourth, Boston and Roosevelt teachers found professional literature usable. Administrators in Roosevelt commented that staff appeared more knowledgeable and more communicative about curricular and classroom management techniques. One validated her collection of data, problem analyses, and ongoing mid-course corrections as a reflection of action research. She found a "spillover into the way that I function in my job." Observations of teams and individuals repeatedly showed that teachers cited research findings and discussed model programs that had been described in scholarly journals.

Fifth, readings outside of education and cross-cultural discussions expanded conceptual horizons for teachers and administrators. A course on Shakespeare and a discussion of alienation gave fresh insights. One teacher commented on how a diverse team enabled its members "to look at the school from a broader perspective." After reading Sarason, an administrator described his current view of change as "evolution, not revolution." A White staff member reported learning "a great deal about inequity . . . in a broader context that I had thought about it before."

Finally, many participants shared their sense of having benefited personally as well as professionally from academic and school-based projects. "The group work has helped me on a more personal level," reported one teacher. Another had "learned and grown from the team base concept." A third added in some jubilation: "It's getting to be fun [despite the] . . . frustrations and defeats . . . there are so many pluses right now that I can't see any negatives." A fourth teacher remarked that she was "getting into the active part of the program. I have received much direction, therefore it is clear in my mind the steps one must take."

Underlying all their comments lay a sense that they as teachers had acted purposefully to set priorities among complex roles and to devise positive programs. They did not experience collaboration with univer-

sities or with other outside organizations as something done to them—
or something done for them. Almost everyone had acted as a leader
and as a follower in their group. Their sense of competence and comfort
related directly to working with their colleagues and interested outsiders
around specific activities that were conceptualized in terms of educational and social issues.

PROFESSIONAL DEVELOPMENT AND PARTNERSHIPS

Most educators begin their career with a desire to help all children to
learn, become independent thinkers, and function productively as
adults. Soon, teachers discover that their ambitions conflict with a reality
of diffuse organizational goals, inadequate resources, and little personal
impact on their school's climate. This sense of powerlessness is not
imposed on teachers by an inappropriate bureaucratic organization or
by their inadequate professional training. According to Lipsky (1980),
teachers and other street-level bureaucrats are inescapably vulnerable
to isolation and mindless routines. Frustrated as their behaviors fall short
of their ideals, most teachers nevertheless facilitate learning for some
students and thereby obtain a degree of job satisfaction.

Because "street-level bureaucrats primarily determine policy implementation" (Lipsky, 1980), school improvement should encourage activities, structures and an ethos fostering staffing empowerment. That
is not a simple challenge. Collaborative activities seem to impose one
more task while offering no respite from the gap between a teacher's
ideals and human capacity. Technical assistance, narrowly construed,
may enable teachers to improve instructional practices, but will not re-
fresh their curiosity or energies. Replacing isolation and diffidence with
positive communication and enthusiasm is difficult or even "mostly
destructive if it is done simply in the name of higher degrees of scrutiny"
(p. 207). The crucial transformation requires "supportive environments
in which peer review is joined to peer support and assistance in the
working out of problems and practices" (p. 206).

In our experience, the group processes of partnerships have generated
at least five important changes in the daily lives of teachers that reward
professionals and emphasize their competence:

1. Teachers are continually reminded of what can be done to improve schools
   rather than being immobilized by all that cannot be changed.
2. Teachers look beyond current practices to what they might do differently.
3. Teachers discover new, unanticipated agendas emerging from their interactions.
4. Teachers sense that the success or failure of personal and organizational
   development lies within their own attitudes, behaviors, purposes and processes.

5. Teachers create new subsettings with shared values and productive interactions as they work together in small groups.

Educational leaders and teachers have long struggled with these issues
of human resource development. Schools have a variety of committees,
task forces, staff meetings, inservice workshops, professional days,
awards and recognition ceremonies, and sometimes merit-pay systems.
Those activities involve insiders who have grown accustomed to the
cultural assumptions and routines of their setting, who have become
locked in a political stalemate, and who have seen the promises of earlier
innovations erode. Outside partners do not magically resolve those
teacher dilemmas, but they often view learning and schools through
different lenses.

In the partnerships we have examined, neither new resources nor
outside expertise alone produced new behaviors and understandings.
Outsiders had no panacea or technical fix for educational problems.
Instead, ongoing activities and discussions stimulated by additional resources and different perspectives empowered teachers to address manageable improvements. Teachers discarded long-held negative attitudes
and renewed their willingness to work with others in win-win contexts.
They recognized their capacity to create a new ethos.

We feel more convinced about partnerships as a vital ingredient for
empowering teachers because it connects so directly with other bodies
of literature about introducing change in schools. As they work together,
teachers and their partners should not ignore what has been learned
about school improvement over the past twenty years. According to
McLaughlin and Marsh's (1978) summaries of the Rand Studies on educational innovation, the following factors are central to establishing
and maintaining effective school-based improvement efforts:

1. Teachers possess the best available clinical expertise—although classroom
realities often fall short of those instructional possibilities.
2. Innovations are implemented in a local setting through adaptive and heuristic
processes.
3. Professional learning is long term and nonlinear.
4. Staff development must be viewed as a program-building process in schools.

In partnerships, issues of communication and positive leadership in
small group activities are particularly salient. In small groups, individual
contributions matter and peer pressures discourage "defectors" and
"free-riders." A positive attitude of mutual benefits helps collaborative
small groups. Because staffs have ordinarily arrived at a stalemate between teachers and administrators, school change is fostered by avoiding
sweeping solutions—such as all teachers will cover writing skills, or all

instruction will involve teams. Alternative programs in a school encourages small groups to transform ideas into practices without requiring uniformity for others.

Collaborative arrangements can expand cultural perspectives and sustain a pluralistic framework of real-world goals. Because small groups may share strong beliefs and agree on specific actions plans, they propel changes. Those factors, however, may cause those teachers to become isolated and ineffective within a larger culture. If small groups become dominant, then difficult adjustments and shifts of power follow as new regularities become established and gain a momentum of their own. Outsiders from parent/community groups, businesses, human service agencies, and institutions of higher education bring different perspectives to small groups. When compatible teachers work toward alternative programs, they often avoid power struggles within their building.

Given positive leadership, school improvement efforts encourage staff involvement around efforts to adopt and adapt something new to serve the needs of all students. Educational reformers should hold ready a "laundry list" of possible ways and steps to improve social climate, curriculum, instructional effectiveness, and communication about goals and objectives. Leaders need to find common elements in dozens of proposals and encourage various groups to pursue their particular "dream" within a broad framework of school purposes and patterns. When these elements are present, then virtually any proposal can, if pursued with enthusiasm, involve teachers in determining their own school climate and thereby dissolve political stalemates.

BUILDING IMPROVEMENT TEAMS

Between 1980 and 1986, the Boston Secondary Schools Project (BSSP) fostered school-based improvement teams in 25 secondary schools located throughout the city. Under court-ordered desegregation, selected high schools in Boston had developed magnet programs intended to attract a racially diverse student population while other buildings gained racial balance through busing. At the same time, reorganization of the city's junior high schools into middle schools also raised issues of curriculum, staffing, and educational purposes. Barriers to communication within each building—such as size, departmental units, and a tradition of independence—suggested a focus on school-based improvement teams with strong support by administrators.

BSSP employed a number of team-building strategies. University faculty served as coaches and facilitators, helping in project development and in the application of research findings to school improvement. They insisted that teachers possessed expert knowledge, especially about instructional strategies and climate issues in their buildings. Some groups produced action research reports. Team members analyzed their school, developed and implemented specific improvement projects, evaluated the success of their efforts, and shared their findings with other teams. Teachers joined voluntarily—in part to satisfy academic requirements and in part to improve their school.

As a consequence, project schools experienced observable changes in specific areas of school organization including decreased dropout rates, higher test scores, greater parent involvement, more discussion among teachers and administrators, and increased readiness among minority students for higher education. Evaluations documented gains during the period BSSP problem-solving teams focused on those areas. Teachers devised new curricular strategies, participated in after-school activities with students, and cooperated with colleagues. Many projects involved non-BSSP teachers, and activities continued after course requirements were completed.

Based on extensive evaluative feedback from BSSP participants at the end of 1981, and again in 1983, teachers and administrators indicated their support for a "team approach" to school improvement (Clark, 1982; Campbell, 1984). One teacher found it "a very effective way to draw many ideas into a single effort, in making better the total educational system. It allows more sharing, more gathering data, effective avenues to experiment in varying educational levels." A second teacher noted staff communication increased "the utilization of varied resources." A third participant thought that teams were a "logical" approach because "one is able to hear others' views, problems, methods, and together a solution can be developed in various ways." A fourth individual argued that "the development of an effective team is very helpful—it really is what makes the university involvement worthwhile."

Although BSSP attracted people interested in school improvement, team building was not simple. Not all participants contributed equally, as many members complained. One teacher remarked, "I believe that the school-based team has been a catalyst for some change in my school—but the team is too small to be truly effective." Another participant argued that "we get to meet a diverse group of people but the diversity sometimes prevents the solutions from getting off the ground."

Effective teams shared certain characteristics. They involved active support by leadership, viewed change as a systemic issue, encouraged members to play a variety of roles, and conceptualized improvement as a series of doable steps (Maloy and Fischetti, 1985). The attitudes of team members and the behavioral characteristics of the team itself reinforced and shaped each other. Some teams discussed personal and organizational goals, and they identified feasible improvement projects. They produced a handbook for students, surveyed parent attitudes toward the school, or designed a new unit on international relations. Less ef-

fective teams avoided frank discussion and misread their project's viability in their setting.

Effective teams involved the school's headmaster or principal as an
active participant. Those teams engaged in substantive school development, involving teachers in larger issues of school climate. More immediately, administrators could provide information and endorsements
that continually clarified roles and made changes practical. When team
members believed their projects would have support, they discussed
ideas and implementation strategies with visible seriousness. Participation by outsiders was welcomed. When school administrators ignored
the teams, there was less openness to self-assessment and less debate
over professional concerns. Those team members expressed bitterness
or condescension toward one another's efforts.

During their first year, most teams experienced periods of confusion
and frustration. Teachers identified specific wrongs and blamed particular individuals. School problems were attributed to personal failings.
Some teams argued that if underachieving students gained "motivation," then discipline issues would disappear. Similarly, if administrators supported teachers, low morale would then be lifted. Gradually
successful teams developed new insights about how systems in schools
operated. Improvement efforts were directed at specific facets of school
organization such as discipline policies, information management, public relations, or staff development. Actions were examined critically, but
not discredited in personal terms.

When teachers first joined the BSSP teams, their roles were negotiated
informally but rarely defined explicitly. In some cases, a building administrator or a particular teacher dominated team proceedings in order
to pursue pet solutions to school problems—a principal wanted a school-
wide discipline policy or a union activist urged a new school governance.
No single agenda or personality dominated the more successful BSSP
teams. Team members undertook a variety of roles, expressed personal
and potentially diverging interests, and openly discussed team goals.
Those teams organized themselves more rapidly and worked with a
greater sense of purpose than those on which one or two people attempted to dictate group objectives.

Finally, all BSSP teams had trouble deciding on a school improvement
project. Some teams struggled to discern a starting point for vague goals
such as improving school climate, increasing parent participation or
raising student achievements. Other teams rejected innovations that
would upset familiar school regularities. Successful teams overcame a
personal conservatism common among experienced teachers and administrators. These teams concentrated on small changes and planning
for success as a way to nurture and extend the team's creativity. Teachers

rejected prepackaged recipes for change and instead worked at a pace that suited their capacity to examine both themselves and their school.

Teachers, administrators, and outside partners constructed their own scenarios of effectiveness or ineffectiveness as they worked together. Dealing openly with disagreements and unfamiliar ideas, team members expressed their ideas and assumptions in meetings, and teachers discovered where other team members stood. Many BSSP teams combined personal attitudes toward change, self-interests, realistic agendas, and mutual benefits to define their own group processes. Outside partners had a special opportunity to help facilitate such self-examinations, and in so doing, they promoted greater school improvement success.

Although negotiations between administrators, teachers, parents and community members on school improvements take time and effort, those agreements also lighten the burden of teachers who have felt isolated and alienated. School improvement involves an ongoing process of identifying priorities, sharing successful coping strategies related to school and district priorities, and communicating positive aspects of school among peers, supervisors, parents and community representatives, business leaders, human service agency personnel, and university faculty.

FOSTERING COLLABORATIVE INNOVATIONS

When collaborations result in group processes that empower teachers, they lead to evolving strategies and new arrangements for educational organizations. But establishing different behavioral regularities in schools has proven difficult. Implementation requires complex steps to build support, seek approval, motivate small group activities, improvise solutions, and reassess goals. In order to encourage teachers, community representatives and others to develop planned school improvements, the staff of the University of Massachusetts/Worcester Staff Development Project devised a checklist so that proposals would have a better chance to attract support and generate useful activities.

First, can proponents present key ideas to outsiders without professional jargon or complex tables of organization? Promising, but complicated, proposals rarely succeed. Many proposals from university researchers focus on narrow refinements that are unimportant to practitioners. Good ideas that require months of preparation and explanation will work only if supported over a sustained period by strong leaders. Proposed changes should be presented in ways that demonstrate benefits to all participants. For instance, a community organization may endorse school volunteers as a way to help students; teachers may want assistance with clerical tasks and tutoring; administrators may seek to encourage community support and to individualize instruction; and superintendents may welcome volunteers as a budgetary savings measure.

Second, does the proposal avoid overpromising results while making clear that the status quo is not satisfactory? Innovations have to justify themselves, evaluate their results, and guarantee success while established programs seldom face such a "zero base budgeting" analysis. Too often collaborative projects have to meet or exceed traditional standards or goals—plus their own. Teachers in new programs have been identified as oddballs, shunted into older facilities, and vaguely associated with unkempt hair and unpopular beliefs. Hence, many school partners quietly support existing arrangements and minimize their association with nontraditional students, teachers or alternative programs.

Third, does the change incorporate new resources or redefine problems as resources? Nothing prohibits youths tutoring other youths; parent volunteers taking over tasks from paid teachers; or large-group instruction and media freeing time for individual consultation or staff development. Businesses, human service agencies and community centers offer intriguing sites for educational activities. Also, those outside institutions suggest different staffing possibilities. During periods of reduced federal support for educational equity and innovation, schools cannot depend on external grants or mandates to induce improvement efforts. Neither can they totally rely on extra commitment and effort from a core of dedicated staff members whose early enthusiasm will predictably give way to frustration and "burnout."

Fourth, does the collaborative activity address instructional services and thus issues of who gets educated? If new efforts reinforce existing power relationships among staff and students, then a stalemated position as depicted by Sarason is likely to prevail both before and after a planned innovation. School partnership activities can provide a range of organizational and instructional modes that may suit the needs of diverse populations. Because some students are educationally cheated due to their skin color, their sex, their appearance, or their physical handicap, then school programs that reinforce social norms will enlist little support from those families now receiving a low-quality education. Inevitably, new resources raise political issues over their allocation.

Fifth, are there ways for outside partners to encourage many small changes without directly challenging the "system"? Contributions from businesses may stimulate unexpected connections and growth while assuring support for the basic curriculum. Joint programs with parent volunteers or a human service agency may loosen, or make humane, the established bureaucratic and alienating environment of most schools. Outsiders may supervise, coach, or teach a class in order to incorporate different skills or encourage small-group instruction.

Sixth, does the proposed change juxtapose different organizational purposes and cultures in a way that reframes perspectives, while allowing potential conflicts to be discussed and managed? When parents, business executives, human service professionals, or college professors enter a school, they often find the rules for maintaining institutional order intrusive and confusing. Although teachers are professionals, they seldom have privacy and autonomy to converse about possible collaborations. Typically, their telephone calls are handled through a switchboard located in a central office. Students, and thus teachers, are tightly scheduled with almost no "free" time. Outside visits, the volunteered resources of a presentation, or an offer of a field trip must fit into that day's schedule.

In order for teachers to interact with other organizations, adjustments must be made to allow different patterns of time use and instructional modes. Partnerships link teachers with other adults whose roles encourage professional autonomy, problem-solving decisions, and responsibility for outcomes. When teachers perceive themselves as empowered professionals, they seek new organizational strategies and structures.

8

Collaborative Structures for School Change

Were our extraterrestrial visitor to observe a hundred classrooms across the United States, ETV might conclude that they are remarkably the same. While teachers talk, children sit at desks or tables and pursue common tasks. The students' age, the month, and time of the day seem to determine the curriculum. Uniformity, predictability and stability of behavior predominate in these rooms. As Albert Shanker commented about the 10,000 new teachers hired by the New York City public schools every year—"the amazing thing is that after three weeks in the classroom you can't tell them apart from the teachers they replaced" (quoted in Deal, 1987, p. 3).

After further observations, ETV might differentiate among urban, rural and suburban schools, large and small districts, or staff and student accents. Depending on one's list of important characteristics, schools may appear sharply different. Racial and class composition vary as do parent involvements, staffing patterns, and student fads. Effective schools advocates have focused attention on a safe, orderly environment and the monitoring of student achievements. Yet most teachers and students understand their schooling as a sequence of similar classroom settings.

Schools are paradoxical organizations. At first glance, they seem bureaucratic and overly controlled through administrative regulations. Indeed, teachers and students often express feelings of powerlessness by referring to the legal and policy guidelines of the system. At the same time, in-depth studies have shown that teachers and principals do, in fact, exercise broad discretion in setting and implementing policies. As Lipsky (1980) pointed out, street-level bureaucrats daily determine school regularities through thousands of professional interactions.

Hence, an observed sameness in this loosely-coupled system apparently follows from the endemic dilemmas of teaching (mainly, coping with groups of students to foster learning by individuals) and a common culture of schools.

Many studies have described a school culture in which people learn common norms, values and regularities of behavior (Waller, 1932; Sarason, 1971, 1982). These social constructions in turn shape the way individuals approach those settings. In their well-known simulation of a prison, a group of social psychologists discovered "how readily we all slipped into our roles, temporarily gave up our identities, and allowed these assigned roles and the social forces in the situation to guide, shape and eventually control our freedom of thought and action" (Zimbardo, Banks, Haney, and Jaffe, 1973, p. 46).

Bronfenbrenner (1979) argued that social roles "evoke perceptions, activities, and patterns of interpersonal relation consistent with role expectations" (p. 92). In schools, for instance, people rarely question the meaning of "student" or "teacher"; and the isolation of education from families and communities has perpetuated those roles. Schools, Bronfenbrenner noted, are "compounds physically and socially insulated from the life of the community, neighborhood, and families the schools purport to serve as well as from the life for which they are supposedly preparing the children" (p. 230). In addition, "classrooms have little or no social identity of their own and little connection with each other or with the school as an active community" (p. 231).

The influence of settings on behavior suggests why empowering teachers through group projects is a necessary but often insufficient step toward reconceptualizing learning for future societies. Ordinary strategies and structures of classrooms have shaped and constrained everyone's thinking about learning. Whatever their preparation, motivation and experience, teachers share a remarkably coherent set of ideas about the purposes of schooling and their behaviors. No wonder beginning teachers frequently report they love teaching but hate school—its organizational mission and bureaucratic structures seem beyond their control. Organizational settings must be reconstructed through group processes and team-building activities that shape new purposes and substructures for school improvement. Effective partnerships support those processes and new perspectives.

FRAMEWORKS FOR ORGANIZATIONAL CHANGE

A prevailing culture of schools has blinded our vision to alternative learning communities. As educational reformers have commented: "Schools are social entities whose function is purposeful learning. As with all social groupings their organizational power is dependent on adherence to *common* sets of values, norms, beliefs, expectations, rules, and sanctions" (Joyce, Hersh, and McKibbin, 1983, p. 24). Those routines strengthen the coherence and economic viability that tie organizational activities together, but they also frustrate responses to new technologies or changing conditions.

Generally, when educators plan school improvements they emphasize rational goals and bureaucratic structures. While acknowledging John Dewey's case for motivating, involving, and validating problem solving within each learner's framework, educational policymakers focus attention on the personnel and the physical resources within their perceived control. They debate over how to manage teachers, texts and classrooms for children from ages five through eighteen in schools that require attendance for 180 days a year. Those reformers believe that by adjusting some feature, imposing more time on academic tasks or a new discipline code, they are "improving" the organization's efficiency. Such adjustments do not question existing school strategies or structures.

Many commentators have applied military and business metaphors to school reforms. In this view "organizations have a staff, line, and chain of command. They develop strategies and tactics" (Weick, 1979, p. 49). Following this line of reasoning, educational leaders throughout this century have urged that schools should be run in tightly coupled, businesslike ways: " . . . the administrative progressives talked increasingly of *problems* to be solved by experts. The rhetoric of reform shifted slowly from a revivalist Protestant-republican ideology to the language of science and business efficiency" (Tyack and Hansot, 1982, p. 107). Their spiritual heirs still seek a management-imposed or expert-determined solution for all schools.

Such metaphors and approaches contradict what is known about organizational development. As Berman (1981) contended, school innovation " . . . consists of three complex organizational subprocesses—mobilization, implementation and institutionalization—that are loosely, not linearly, coupled" (p. 264). In the twentieth century, schools have routinized roles and formal structures. The task of conceptualizing alternative educational arrangements can be a "near-impossible one for most people because it confronts them with the necessity of changing their thinking, then changing their actions, and finally, changing the overall structure of the setting" (Sarason, 1971, p. 13).

Bolman and Deal (1984) have described organizations from four different perspectives—human resources, structural, political, and symbolic. From a human resources frame, improving the organization involves changing people through training, coaching, and personnel shifts. From a structural frame, organizational change means restructuring goals, technology, and tables of organization on the assumption that form and function are rationally related. In political terms, reform involves a redistribution of power among shifting coalitions of groups formed by their self-interests and past interactions. Within a symbolic frame, change follows as leaders refocus meanings, values and visions to create a new organizational ethos.

School reformers need all four frames to recognize the incredible complexities of human resources, strategies and structures, power struggles, and cultural meanings present in every organizational change. "Each theoretical approach—individual, structural, political, and symbolic—has its own ideas, language, assumptions, prophecies, and prescriptions for changing organizations" (Deal, 1986, p. 122). Each approach sustains metaphors for viewing processes of change:

Change is like a revival tent or training ground where individuals are saved or new skills learned to meet new challenges. Change is like a set of tinkertoys where roles and relationships are rearranged into a stronger, more workable design. Change is like a jungle where beasts, herds, and flora compete for scarce resources and struggle for survival. Change is like carnival or theater, an activity in which deep-seated values are dramatized and transformed. (Deal, 1986, p. 122)

Partnerships are voluntary and sustained interactions among organizations or their subunits. School improvement through collaboration involves organizations that are small, local, particularistic, and diversely led on the one hand; on the other hand, their functions and leadership are formed by an institutional culture and national social functions. Outside organizations such as parent and community groups, businesses, human service agencies, and institutions of higher education are likewise both idiosyncratic and shaped by their strategies and structural commonalities.

Interorganizational activities foster a self-consciousness about roles and structures that is essential for meaningful school improvements. Partnerships need to establish a substructure that can make decisions (governance), sustain activities (management), and renegotiate evolving purposes (leadership). According to Lieberman, partnerships are "organizational 'third worlds,' " and Goodlad added that "the most significant changes occur when two cultures bump against one another" (Olson, 1987, pp. 1, 5). Those dynamics of cooperation and conflict will generate "noisy" communications, "messy" organizational charts, and "confusing" transformations of purposes.

A NEW STRUCTURE FOR TEACHER EDUCATION

Collaborations open opportunities for new substructures that support alternative activities that are partially outside a school's culture. Traditionally, public schools and universities define cooperative components of teacher education programs as a straightforward exchange. Institutions of higher education place interns with public school teachers who allow a university student into their classroom, and they offer tuition waivers for the cooperating teacher. In essence, practicum sites are exchanged for courses related to professional growth or advanced degrees.

Initially, those transactions carry a sense of purpose and relationship-building with schools. As internships become routine, few people at the school or university level recall how and why the original arrangements were established. University students observe the class for a specified number of hours and then they instruct under the supervision of the cooperating teacher. For the duration of their internship, they operate within the school's rules and norms. Similarly, when taking university courses, supervising teachers become graduate students—facing lines at registration, assignments in the library, and semester schedules that ignore their professional responsibilities.

Under those arrangements, organizational interactions flow in one direction—individuals from an organization act within the others' structure. If a cooperating teacher's classroom or school year is difficult, there is little time or energy to build a supportive relationship with an intern. Differences are not ordinarily attributed to organizational patterns or systemic problems. Disputes are blamed on personality conflicts, inadequate supervision, or weak academic backgrounds among those choosing careers in education. Deeper questions about what constitutes an optimal mix of classroom and field experiences seldom arise. Renegotiations are foreclosed by assumptions of conventional hierarchies, state requirements, and existing programmatic regularities.

Interactive partnerships may promote new structures for preparing teachers. For example, the Math English Science Technology Education Project (MESTEP) involves the University of Massachusetts at Amherst with high-technology firms and school systems in the eastern part of the state. MESTEP began in 1982 when public school administrators met with officials from the Massachusetts High Technology Council, the School of Education, and the initial business partner—Digital Equipment Corporation. Responding to a perceived shortage of mathematics and science teachers, the partners recruited talented college graduates for a combined fifteen-month certification/master's degree program with interships in both businesses and schools.

In adding a business partner, school and university administrators reconsidered many typical teacher education program activities (Clark et al., 1984). During their first summer in the project, participants combine certification practicums with seminars emphasizing instructional skills and the educational applications of computers. In order to simplify the yearlong arrangements in schools and firms, interns are paired, usually by subject area. During their corporate interships, participants develop educational software, edit textbooks, assist in company education programs, or design new approaches to information management. While teaching, they follow a normal schedule with two or three separate class preparations, study hall and cafeteria duties, and, in some cases, extracurricular assignments. In the second summer, they learn evaluation and assessment techniques and complete courses required for certification.

Developing interships and interorganizational cooperation has directly affected MESTEP's recruitment efforts. This unique program has produced great interest among graduating college seniors. Over 1,400 people inquired about the program during the 1986–87 school year, and three times as many people applied as were accepted. Applicants—each of whom had other job options available to her or him after graduation—have listed their key reasons for considering teaching as a career: intensity of the program, immediate responsibilities for teaching, linkages to industry, and paid internships (J. Fischetti, personal communication, April 1987).

MESTEP's participants allowed the strategies and structures of the program to emerge in new ways. The project's private sector network has expanded to include Bank of Boston, Cullinet, Data General, General Motors, Hewlett-Packard, Houghton Mifflin, IBM, Prime Computer, Spinnaker Software, and New England Telephone. Secondary English was added as a certification area. The Fund for the Improvement of Postsecondary Education has supported recruitment and follow-up contacts with graduates. Both public schools and firms have taken on university instructional roles by supervising internships and providing part of the academic coursework needed for certification. Project planners created a coordinating committee to promote linkages between organizations, to consider modifications in university and school curriculums, and to facilitate new roles for teachers, faculty and industry participants.

This committee served as a forum for issues raised by rethinking teacher preparation. Business representatives supported pay for interns to build accountability and credibility of MESTEP within industry circles. That decision pressured school systems to follow suit, and that salary altered their understanding of the roles of teachers and students. Seventy MESTEP students view themselves as new leaders in the areas of math and science education, 55 able teachers in the public schools have ongoing clinical relationships with students, and 40 company personnel serve as teachers and researchers concerned with instructional applications of computer technology.

As a small project with a distinct identity, MESTEP could test new arrangements, tap new sources of potential teachers, and introduce new behaviors within all three organizational cultures. The four frames proposed by Bolman and Deal (1984) illuminate how each partner gained. The excitement generated by creating a new setting encouraged human resource development. Strategies and structures had to be connected afresh to accommodate the interests of business firms. The project carried clout and obtained outside funding in part due to the political and economic power of the High Technology Council. Finally, the association of computers with math and science teaching created powerful symbols that brought the project national recognition and connected participants to a mission of purposeful innovation.

CREATING MANY BEST SYSTEMS

As we have urged schools to foster loosely structured collaborations with parent/community organizations, businesses, human service agencies, and colleges, we have heard lingering objections from those who suspect educational reforms should be managed by experts. Schooling involves complex and interrelated systems directed by professionals toward both equal opportunities and the highest level of training for societal elites. Who would choose anyone but the best surgeon or the best teacher? Over the past two decades, reformers have described the development of educational bureaucracies with distinctly ambivalent feelings (Tyack, 1974; Katz, 1971).

In broad terms, of course, schools have adopted a recognizable order for most instruction, although individuals may learn quickly or lag behind the prescribed curriculum. Across the United States and internationally, schools follow a similar curricular pattern. Addition precedes multiplication, and algebra precedes geometry. Teachers emphasize vocabulary, mathematical techniques, and other "testable" skills because they assume standardized achievement results "demonstrate" effectiveness of school inputs. Public pressures for minimum competency tests reflect a common perception that teachers as well as their students should know certain things. County-wide systems and urban districts have encouraged standardized management of similar school buildings filled with identical classrooms that discourage variations and adaptation to local or new conditions.

Although schools do process and differentiate individual learners to some degree, what John Meyer (1978) has identified as "macro-sociological effects" may have more importance. Formal education serves as a key social institution in modern economies. Education has become "a central element in the table of organization of society, constructing competencies and helping to create professions and professionals" (p. 55). Schooling serves a legitimization function. It acts "as a system of institutionalized rites transforming social roles through powerful initiation ceremonies and as an agent transforming society by creating new classes of personnel with new types of authoritative knowledge" (p. 56).

In that context, the quality of one's schooling matters less than the years attended, degrees received, and the responses engendered by the presumed social significance of that accreditation (Jencks et al., 1972). In today's world, it sounds like uncommon sense to suggest that many competent people have not completed high school and that many foolish notions are purveyed by those with earned doctorates. Academic courses and special examinations are required to practice law or to teach. Whether the taught and tested knowledge is directly job-related may be largely beside the point that the system validates social roles:

> Educational systems themselves are thus, in a sense, ideologies. They rationalize in modern terms and remove from sacred and primordial explanations the nature and organization of personnel and knowledge in modern society. They are, presumably, the effects of the reorganization of modern society around secular individualism which is a main theme of Marx and Weber. (Meyer, 1978, p. 66)

Accordingly, education as an institution may serve as a potent myth—powerful because it is so widely believed.

That social construction of reality—which is fostered by educators and which, in turn, shapes the social roles of schools—suggests both despair and hope about educational reforms. Everyone may recognize loose connections between sense and schooling, "but in hiring and promoting, in consulting the various magi of our time, and in ordering our lives around contemporary rationality, we carry out our parts in a drama in which education is authority" (Meyer, 1978, pp. 75–76). Presumedly, graduates of elite institutions are best qualified to define school reforms. Yet based on their families' positive experiences in schools, those same individuals have a vested interest in maintaining the current system's major functions—as well as its constructed reality.

This sociological perspective suggests why issues of access and equity have so agitated educational debates. Schools have enabled individuals to acquire skills and experiences relevant to leadership roles; but, more broadly, the educational system has authorized certain professions and thus a social and economic hierarchy. Urban school failures have lent credibility to persistent, pervasive and powerful patterns of White racism. By accepting existing patterns of discrimination—although allowing a handful of individuals to earn degrees as the exceptions that demonstrate the force of the rule—schools have legitimized social inequities.

An egalitarian educational system would challenge the social legitimization function of schools. Not all Americans would applaud if urban teachers shared information and skills that enabled poor and minority students to take their place as productive workers and responsible citizens in a more equal society. In fact, no single program is likely to overcome the "over-caused" cycle of poverty and discrimination affecting urban schools. Their students endure community disamenities, inadequate housing, hunger, ill health, family disruptions, poorly prepared teachers, culturally biased instructional materials, racial and class discrimination, and a sense of hopelessness. Were schools truly fair and meritocratic, those conditions might aptly be blamed on their victims. In a society permeated with White racism, those conditions tend to perpetuate poverty for Blacks and prejudice among relatively advantaged groups.

In an uncertain world, there are good reasons for adopting less efficient, loosely coupled systems that can adapt to future options. For example, unless one knows what race will be run and when, a meritocratic track program can scarcely select between a sprinter or a long distance runner for intensive training. As Weick (1982) has indicated, education as a loosely coupled system has oten advanced in many directions at once, thereby frustrating efficiency experts or those with a cure-all. At the same time, it preserved options and flexibility to meet contingencies from new mandates or demands. Till we know what kind of world we will create, schools have to recognize diverse skills, appreciate cultural differences, and prepare youth for adaptation and continuous learning as adults.

This recognition of diversity and tolerance for programs that may lead up dead-end streets cannot condone systematic educational failures for some groups. For too long, educators have tolerated discrimination reflecting unequal distributions of economic, political and social power, especially those afflicting low-income, minority, female, and handicapped students. Although the initial impact of bureaucratic school systems considerably expanded opportunities for a quality education and thus brought greater equality, that system today often blocks the professional capacity of teachers. When society's legitimization system reinforces and perpetuates poverty and discrimination, teachers find that meritocracy is subverted and thus their professional role is corrupted.

ALTERNATIVE STRUCTURES

In quite practical ways, school improvement partnerships can reduce bureaucratic barriers to new behavioral regularities. Outside organizations offer not only their perspective and additional resources but also a crucial legitimization of alternative schedules, locations and programs. Open agreements, reaffirmed in contracts and public statements, validate differences from the prevailing school culture. They allow educators to reconceptualize their strategies and structures. Although many partnerships have supported elite groups, nevertheless they have raised issues of fairness to a conscious level. Not surprisingly, MESTEP has recruited more minority students than its traditional counterpart on campus.

The way people in organizations envision their purposes and strategies defines their perceived problems. If a principal believes that the school should create a safe and orderly environment for regularly scheduled academic courses, then extracurricular activities, field trips, staff development workshops, lovely spring days, and both talented and alienated students pose challenges for the school's schedule. Yet many alternative schools have demonstrated how those same factors contribute enormously to intense learning. Projects in the local community on a fresh May afternoon can allow students and teachers to reengage with each other, thereby discovering unforeseen skills. Outside the building, interdisciplinary explorations can proceed beyond a 42-minute class period.

Although schools commonly adjust their routine schedules and use off-site facilities, they usually regard those events as exceptional. Collaborations can justify out-of-school activities. For instance, the Worcester East Middle School utilized space in a neighborhood center, Friendly House, to serve adolescents who could not cope with tightly scheduled classes for a whole day. Under the guidance of a caring teacher, many students managed to stay in school, keep pace with academic subjects, and develop self-esteem. The casual yet busy atmosphere of Friendly House was not disturbed when students engaged in a variety of individual assignments or a spontaneous game of basketball. As the relationship grew, the youths served meals for senior citizens and developed a sense of involvement with their community center.

Alternative schools such as the well-known Parkway Program in Philadelphia illustrated the potential for enhancing learning by breaking down commonly accepted norms for schools. The program's founding leader, John Bremer, insisted that

no change will be of any significance unless the social organization of education is totally changed, that is unless the system itself is changed. Nothing less will do, for it is the whole system that defines the nature and function of the parts. As a consequence, imaginative and fruitful ways of helping students to learn become, ultimately, only new ways for subordinating the student to the present system, only another way of keeping the student under control. (Bremer and Moschzisker, 1971, p. 11)

By using space and volunteered instructors in Philadelphia's central business district, Bremer saved the costs of a new building and discovered a variety of ways to create an exciting learning community.

The Parkway Program developed a number of tactics to overcome existing routines. Students were not assigned to Parkway. Instead, they applied on a four-line form and obtained permission from at least one parent. When over 2,000 applications arrived for 120 places, Bremer held a public lottery designed to assure a racial mix approximating that of the city. Known as the school without walls, Parkway only lacked its own walls, "for it utilized the buildings within Philadelphia as it needed them and could negotiate them" (Bremer and Moschzisker, 1971, p. 19). Bremer insisted that "when students entered Parkway, they entered a program, not a school; a process, not a place; an activity, not a location" (p. 21). Courses were taught by "the faculty, interns, businessmen, parents, students, librarians, curators and individual volunteers" (p. 24).

School improvement efforts naturally attempt something new and the more their approaches vary from school regularities, the more questions and doubts must be answered. Alternative schools are ordinarily motivated or accompanied by a healthy critique of educational bureaucracies—those regulations, norms and cultural patterns that seem to limit experimentation, individualization, and programs to address needs of underserved students. Yet those alternative structures need some legitimization from outside organizations. By 1971, the Parkway Program cited cooperation and support from over 37 community organizations, 34 firms, 11 colleges or universities, and 16 human service agencies.

Parkway responded to concerns about the lack of relevance of academics to urban life by offering a course taught by an editor from a Philadelphia newspaper. No editorial complained about the uncertified instructor. In that sense, legitimization was a two-way street because it demonstrated that businesses, agencies, institutions of higher education, and community organizations did care about a learning community and future societies in practical ways. Because the larger myth of schools and society as a meritocratic placement system has grown too familiar to be questioned, collaborations can support smaller, more understandable connections that may build a new legitimacy.

Linkages between alternative programs and large organizations can be tricky to handle because groups that have separated themselves from public schools resist joining another bureaucratic system. Yet the Greenfield project, English High School and Worcester East Middle School gained legitimacy from their association with appropriate outside organizations—school volunteers, John Hancock Life Insurance, and Friendly House. Responding to low-income and minority youths who left schools, Street Academies drew support from the Urban League, local businesses, community groups, and, usually, the school district. Many on-site career or vocational programs cooperate with local businesses for placements and for subsequent employment opportunities. Nontraditional schools benefit from linkages with institutions of higher education till their graduates demonstrate a track record of college acceptances.

When educational reformers recognize that a bureaucratic school system fundamentally conflicts with individualization and with professional empowerment of teachers, then outside linkages make sense within individual, structural, political, and symbolic frames. Community groups, businesses, human service agencies, and institutions of higher education can offer volunteers, funds and ideas while providing learning sites and adult interactions. As alternative programs struggle against the schools' bureaucratic structures, they obtain legitimization from outside organizations, although too close connections seemingly replace one value system with another. Hence, collaborations ordinarily bring political issues to the surface because alternative programs have to describe and defend their new practices. Finally, attempts to motivate and sustain a new organizational structure require a clear mission, symbols, heroes, and charismatic leadership.

EVOLVING ORGANIZATIONS

Despite recent efforts to describe schools operating in a nonrational context (Barth, 1980; Boyer, 1983; Comer, 1980; Goodlad, 1984; Lighfoot, 1983; Sarason, 1982), we lack a satisfactory vocabulary for comprehending organizational change. The following propositions suggest some intuitively practical guidelines for partners to use in reconceptualizing educational systems. Specific features of partnerships incorporate multiple visions and redefine problems in ways that can promote innovation in schools. By understanding those conditions, partnerships remain manageable and capable of evolution while incorporating diverse groups within their problem definitions. In so doing, they sustain legitimacy for alternative learning communities.

First, make issues ill-structured so that the "problems" become resources. Two organizations seldom agree to work together through a substructure that responds to shared concerns unless each group has some dissatisfaction with existing conditions. Typically, that discontent is perceived ambiguously or uncertainly, and possible responses to such ill-structured problems involve new voices, strategies, and structures that upset established power arrangements.

When organizations involved in school improvement collaborations approach issues as "well-structured," they seek traditional or "more of the same" solutions. For example, teachers and parents might consider working together on issues of early adolescence that seem problematic. Youths aged ten to thirteen develop quickly, manifesting rapid shifts in their physical, social, and intellectual behaviors. Adults can wear themselves out responding to that search for identity or capitalize on their youthful energy and curiosity. Students who have demonstrated readiness for high school work might intern on a part-time basis in local community service agencies. Others who lack basic social or academic skills could receive individualized instruction from teachers or community members.

In most organizational environments a broad ethos—"this is the way we do things around here"—dictates what constitutes appropriate or inappropriate proposals for change (Peters and Waterman, 1982). System-altering ideas often come from people who are considered "oddballs," "loners," or have been otherwise separated from the mainstream of organizational experience (Deal and Kennedy, 1982). The particular contribution of partnerships is their potential to foster a substructure that taps resources from both organizations in mutually beneficial interchanges that generates multiple insights. Because many basic human problems are ill-structured when viewed from current paradigms, this reframing of issues encourages the reflection required to renegotiate public agreements on the purposes of schooling.

Second, frame issues in shared and win-win terms during interorganizational negotiations. Interactive partnerships involve continual bargaining and hence chronically raise issues about who has benefited most or contributed least. Organizational leaders have to emphasize mutual benefits for participants while hoping that interactive processes will indirectly serve larger institutional purposes. Ordinarily a proposed transaction raises old disagreements and lingering doubts about commitment and capacity. Obliged to, ought to, want to motivations and different priorities complicate negotiations till some shared activities emerge. Yet often both outside volunteers and students benefit from their interactions and strengthen institutional linkages.

In 1984, undergraduates from the University of Massachusetts at Amherst began tutoring Cambodian, Vietnamese, and Amerasian students at a local secondary school. Those who planned the project—principally a university faculty member, a graduate student, a secondary administrator, and an English as a Second Language teacher—had to overcome historical mistrusts about the university. Because the lives of Southeast Asians had been profoundly complicated by war, family breakup, and adjustments to Amherst, no one knew whether undergraduate tutors could help. Some assumed the university could not adjust bureaucratically. Since then, a dozen undergraduates have tutored 25 to 35 junior and senior high school students from Southeast Asia. Both tutors and their students describe their interactions positively. High school staff regard undergraduates as useful and responsible. Parents praised the project; the state's Department of Education cited it as an exemplary component of transitional bilingual education; and in 1986, the project received an Innovative Programming Award from the National University Continuing Education Association and the American College Testing Program. Although minuscule in terms of the university and the school system, the project's payoffs have created a more favorable attitude toward future interchanges.

Third, create organizational shells characterized by discretion and flexibility among participants. If partnerships are to evolve beyond an exchange of services, they must devise ways to manage interactive decisions. When goals of cooperation are vague, like that of school improvement, then project planners can scarcely specify means and outcomes in advance. Yet when everything seems open to debate, teachers and outsiders flounder about in a search for practical steps toward planned action and appropriate resources. Hence, partnership arrangements usually propose structural shells that create governance bodies or foci for shared activities. Representative councils structure negotiations without foreclosing ongoing input from participants. Likewise, an agreement to support a resource center may direct volunteers who want to advance their particular interests and goals.

Partnerships ordinarily establish governance bodies with representatives from the major parties and a modest advisory role. Such councils or boards allow voice to each major interest. Previously unrepresented groups such as parents, students, or local businesses and agencies gain input into program planning, personnel decisions, resource allocations, or evaluation criteria. Often the juxtaposition of outsiders' concerns reframes educational problems. Parents and other community adults may attract resources from contributors not open to teachers. Human service agencies may offer special training on sensitive issues such as sex education or drug abuse while businesses might share their knowledge about computers.

Shells also can organize activities for groups whose direction must be determined later. The Worcester/University of Massachusetts Staff Development proposal called for a parent/teacher resource center in each of the schools served by the project. Since project planners wanted teachers and community members to determine their own initiatives, they could not specify in advance what activities would meet those objectives. In creating a space and acquiring materials, teachers and parents established joint ownership and began to define agendas for strengthening the curriculum. Project organizers allocated funds to a parent/teacher council that decided on appropriate materials and activities at the resource centers.

As with many features of collaborative projects, formal governance procedures are generally less significant than the opportunities for informal interchanges among participants. A normal practice of open discussions prior to actions allows participants to introduce vital information in a timely fashion. Hence, governance should be viewed as a shell that facilitates information exchanges without hindering useful initiatives. Planning a partnership requires a careful division of decision-making responsibility with most details left for those most affected by them.

Fourth, develop substructures with a life of their own separate from core organizations. Mature organizations evolve slowly, but substructures created by partnerships can explore new strategies, resources and goals. In Parkway, John Bremer insisted on clusters of 120 students with distinct identities in order to assure their voice in local decisions. MESTEP's coordinating council, BSSP's advisory board, and informal or personal associations in the John Hancock/English High School or Roosevelt projects act as a decision-making or implementation body occupying a middle ground between the two sponsoring organizations.

Likewise, teacher centers or educational collaboratives establish a decision-making body responsive to school, university and community needs. Previously, teacher development was controlled either by districts or institutions of higher education. When under a school's aegis, inservice activities seldom carried graduate credit, lacked coherence over time, and often served administrative agendas. When offered as graduate courses, schedules and subjects were determined by universities and seldom fit needs and time frames of teachers. The institutional imperatives of the dominant organization prevailed so that university courses were cancelled when low enrollments indicated insufficient tuition fees. Teacher centers have established a middle ground with enough institutional status so that satisfactory compromises do not have to be renegotiated each year.

Collaborative substructures thus proceed through definable stages: Inception involves operational steps to create a name and assign a contact person within each institution. Growth of mutually beneficial activities leads significant individuals in both organizations to recognize the partnership's independent substructure. The partnership organization may succeed, fail, progress, mutate, or decline depending on the interactions, negotiations, and interpretations of the people involved. Regardless of their life span or pattern of growth, partnerships need a life of their own in order to examine multiple realities, ponder ill-structured problems, and take risks unacceptable to mature organizations.

9

Leadership and Management for Collaborative Growth

An exemplary collaboration between Queens College and Louis Armstrong Middle School resulted from a "chance conversation" between the president of the college and the chancellor of the New York City schools (Trubowitz et al., 1984, p. 29). In Greenfield, playground construction funded through a federal program facilitated interactions among community members and teachers. The Roosevelt project built on longstanding personal relationships. MESTEP emerged from a series of professional connections and informal meetings among school, business, and university leaders that continued till people decided to work together on improving preparation for mathematics and science teachers.

Many projects begin in unplanned ways and evolve in unanticipated directions. A school program for homeless children in Worcester depended on relationships established through using dining and gymnasium facilities at a nearby community center. A school in Holyoke purchased bilingual instructional materials after staff from an environmental education agency conducted a series of experiential lessons for third and sixth graders in both Spanish and English. New curriculum units on Afro-American history were planned by teachers in Springfield after classes from their school had visited an exhibit on Africa at the city's science museum.

These stories are useful reminders to leaders who are planning, managing and assessing partnerships. Fortunate circumstances and timely occurrences are natural parts of collaborative efforts. Joint activities among people and organizations involve unexpected happenings and outcomes. School partnerships appear whimsical or personal at the outset, haphazard and unpredictable in their growth, and difficult to assess at various points in their life cycle. Leadership for collaborative growth is situational, contingent and interactive. This does not mean successful leaders behave whimsically or nonrationally. Rather, they take advantage of serendipitous conjunctions and adopt flexible approaches to organizations as political and symbolic systems.

Because partnerships usually address ill-structured problems, leaders cannot adopt rational structures and bureaucratic procedures with linear steps for meeting well-understood objectives. A group may set out to reduce academic failures and end up addressing social and self-esteem concerns for early adolescents. In a way, the difficulty of establishing accountability in an organization characterized by multiple goals and approaches makes it more important for leaders to assess and evaluate what happened and for whom. By describing contexts, needs, processes, and interactions, leaders come to understand the meaning of school improvement for participants. Thus project assessments and evaluations are not a report card that records whether one passed or failed at school improvement, but an individualized record that indicates what outcomes one has achieved and how.

Hence, leaders of school partnerships use assessments and evaluations not to hold participants accountable—after all their efforts are typically volunteered—but to describe to both outsiders and participants the meaning of their achievements. In that context, teachers talking with each other and learning of their isolation and frustrations with bureaucracies may establish a common experience for better teamwork on a curricular or management issue. Or teacher feedback may indicate that the value of a group exercise did not lie in the consensus arrived at but the feeling of group empowerment. Furthermore, a loosely structured evaluation can clarify those unanticipated outcomes and chance linkages that strengthen most projects. Good leaders will use documentation and summary reports to promote new cultural values through heroes and honored achievements.

LEADERSHIP FOR EDUCATIONAL CHANGE

Initiating and supporting voluntary responses to ill-structured problems by involving insiders and outsiders in group activities requires leadership skills of a particular sort. Management cannot be bureaucratic, hierarchical, objective-driven, and tightly controlled for individual accountability—although those techniques may help to organize small-group activities and to inform the larger system. Leaders can articulate a compelling vision of how to address students' needs and serve larger social purposes. Leaders can juxtapose perspectives, encourage diversity, allow the freedom to fail, and welcome both innovations and reinventions of old ideas. Leaders can assess gains in the school climate—

most directly in loosening those forces that inhibit professional growth among teachers and organizational development within schools.

Typically, leadership proposals have focused on rational efforts to unblock human resources through team building or to rearrange bureaucratic structures. Deal (1986) urged considerations of political and cultural frameworks. Organizational change invariably "will have its winners and losers, its contests and conflicts, its exchanges of power" (p. 118). Although political struggles involve interests and negotiating tactics, they are never wholly rational. Schools involve an ethos, an accepted collection of dramas, ceremonies and norms that hold the staff and students together. Outsiders may identify its transmission through rites, rituals, stories, and heroes; but no one can predictably redesign a new organizational ethos or necessarily associate particular cultural manifestations with heightened productivity. Hence, leaders should have the flexibility to respond in an empathetic, highly organized, powerful, or charismatic manner as the situation requires.

As an elementary principal, Roland Barth (1980) discovered that ambiguity and uncertainty required flexibility on the part of school leaders:

Enlisting and assisting the diverse parties involved in the life of a school—teachers, parents, students—in a coalition each member of which respects that same diversity in others, is a larger part of making the process work. The life of pluralistic institutions rests upon the recognition that respect for any person's uniqueness and integrity depends upon that person's honoring all others in the same way. (p. 218)

Political skills, he found, grew in importance when coalitions included outside partners in a common vision of educational purposes.

In-depth interviews with principals have emphasized "the significance of school culture, the ethos of teachers as a group, and the larger social and political context within which the school is embedded" (Blumberg and Greenfield, 1986, p. 239). A leader's workday "is largely social, and interpersonal communication with individuals and small groups is the medium through which the principal works at the 'craft' of administering the school" (p. 238). Effective principals "engage in a kind of running battle with the school culture and what one accomplishes as a principal is constrained by the limits of culture and context on the range of what is possible in that school situation" (p. 239). What ties all the pieces together, according to Blumberg and Greenfield, is "value leadership, vision, and the capacity to exercise 'moral' imagination" (p. 239).

Recently, educational researchers have looked at schools in a "non-rational world." Given a core mission to facilitate learning within a pleasant environment, educational leaders must cope with unsystematic conditions:

- Goals can be multiple, competing, contradictory, ambiguous, and promoted by a variety of interest groups.
- Decision making is closely tied to goal definition. . . . Final decisions are made from a limited range of options in a last-minute flurry of negotiations and compromise.
- Power is an open-ended entity, available throughout the organization to those who have access to resources.
- The external environment is volatile and unpredictable, it intrudes at all points in the process. (Patterson, Purkey, and Parker, 1986, p. 114)

To manage partnerships in a nonrational world, leaders need "a more functional and holistic way of thinking about organizations" (p. 116). They must recognize multiple realities and a range of interests and motivations in order to anticipate both cooperation and conflict. They must simultaneously consider multiple perspectives and alternative solutions within specified settings. In particular, "effective leaders must have a clear understanding of culture's role in educational organizations. Only then can they effectively employ strategies to alter the culture and build effective structures" (p. 117).

There are five particular aspects for leadership that we have identified based on our experiences in working with school improvement partnerships:

1. creating inducements for voluntary contributions—because time and human interaction are costly and not easily justified when problems are ill-structured;
2. incorporating insights from insiders and outsiders, experts, laypeople, and consumers because cultural insights are fostered by multiorganizational perspectives and an array of plausible alternatives;
3. empowering small-group processes and activities within an encompassing vision of educational reform;
4. assessing program development in ways that both help participants improve their activities and share a sense of empowerment; and
5. evaluating collaborations in terms of processes that relate to an open, loosely structured, and self-conscious organizational climate.

PARTNERSHIPS AS A CATALYST FOR VOLUNTARISM

Given some encouragement, ideas and resources from school leaders and outsiders, collaborative activities rely primarily on volunteered support. If immediate interchanges are structured so that individuals can mutually benefit, then some members from each organization will want to participate in activities that serve both personal and institutional goals. Formal and informal communication from recognized leaders is required to legitimize new activities, and to establish boundaries around acceptable change.

There are significant management and leadership strategies for motivating and organizing volunteers. A menu of useful activities has to be scheduled, advertised, and encouraged. Leaders have to respond quickly to information whether voiced or reflected in participation rates. Dull or irrelevant meetings or work groups will soon lose membership. Thus, partnerships require a subsidy of managerial time to present and structure activities for others. Partnership staff must be readily available to listen and convey information to others in ways that might be described as troubleshooting or crisis prevention.

Leaders must also connect staff and organizational developments because such activities create payoffs that extend beyond specific skills or formal job descriptions. Most organizations adjust to meet changing conditions through on-the-job learning by their staff that is largely peripheral to their work—or through continuing education voluntarily undertaken for personal advancement. Adults are rapid learners and effective teachers of others when they are recognized as self-directed, experienced, competent, ready to acquire relevant information, and active problem-solvers (see Knowles, 1978, pp. 55–59). Partnerships engage workers in explorations of new strategies and structures as well as their personal goals.

Leaders who support alternatives may obtain volunteers without mandating system-wide policies and procedures. For instance, in order to meet the schedules of full-time employees, institutions of higher education "will have to adjust scheduling and curriculum time frames for more intensive instruction and learn to teach adults more effectively. This can be done by selected professors interested in particular subjects; it hardly requires an across-the-board change in the college structure" (Eurich, 1985, p. 126). In our experience, projects readily identified staff members who willingly accommodated a different time frame or wanted to explore alternative instructional formats.

Collaborative projects involve substantial management costs for the coordination required to match needs with resources so that teachers' time would not be wasted on irrelevant courses and unusable techniques. An assessment of costs and benefits from the Worcester/University of Massachusetts Staff Development Project revealed the commitment of time by faculty, administrators and support staff to learn what teachers need and can benefit from during school partnerships (Emery and Jones, 1982). Providing pertinent instruction on-site must meet the interrelated requirements and expectations of public schools, universities, and parents/community groups whose support is essential for the long-run success of the program.

The project director, academic coordinator, and staff assistant at the university worked with an academic advisory board, gathering ideas and helping to shape specific courses to meet the aspirations of teachers as identified through periodic needs assessments. After courses were set and scheduled a second stage of orientation took place. New instructors were informed about the project's participants, procedures, immediate past history, related courses, short- and long-term expectations, and support for extra services for students. Most instructors still made mid-course revisions of materials and expectations; and the project encouraged those changes.

A simple illustration suggests the relative costs of management and volunteered time involved in adult education. Assuming a wage of $8 an hour, which was a fairly standard hourly rate, an inservice course for twenty teachers would "cost" $160 per hour. In most partnerships, teachers have foregone those earnings and, in fact, they usually paid their tuition as well. A three-hour seminar, meeting fourteen times a semester, would mean $6,720 of foregone earnings. Graduate courses require two hours of preparation for each class hour, so that a seminar for teachers represented a voluntary contribution of more than $20,000 in their time. On that basis, the Teacher Corps staff development effort in Worcester stimulated more than $600,000 in "donated" time by teachers.

Those large opportunity costs for adult learners suggest a chronic waste in many graduate programs. Instruction may be effective and the ideas and techniques introduced capable of leading to achievement gains on the part of elementary and secondary students. But if teachers are discouraged from trying out curricular changes, then new skills as well as the foregone earnings by teachers are dissipated. The school district may pay higher salaries for additional professional qualifications while its own climate hinders meaningful instructional or management innovations.

Leaders who encourage voluntary activities must avoid imposing their objectives while creating a sense of collaborative possibilities. In opening opportunities for new perspectives and resources, they propose "shells" and activities that allow for development and then manage those changes through continually communicating suggestions, possibilities, and policy limitations. Ideally, school leaders can share a vision that connects learning to feasible improvements in schools.

EXPERTS AND OUTSIDE PERSPECTIVES

School leaders turn to outside consultants or experts to provide staff and organizational development assistance, but the results have often been disappointing. As McLaughlin and Marsh (1978) noted, the "needs of a staff are not always predictable or synchronized with scheduled training sessions," and "staff often cannot perceive what they need to know until the need arises." Thus, while "it was better to use no outside consultants than to use poor ones," even "good consultants actually diminished project outcomes in some cases." Finally, because the principal is "chiefly responsible for establishing the school's educational policies and philosophy," a change project that was in "agreement with the school's general operating style would be more likely to be sustained than one that was not" (p. 78).

School leadership must be construed in "broad, institutional terms, not narrow, special-project terms" (McLaughlin and Marsh, 1978, p. 85). Leaders who are effective realize that they must encourage school people to work with external individuals and groups to "reinvent the wheel" as a way to aid implementation of new ideas into a school setting. When consultants offer a technical fix or esoteric expertise they diminish motivation among teachers to tap their own clinical skills. Consultants from industry, universities, agencies or private firms can present new information and techniques in many areas, but they help most when they inspire and motivate in-school individuals and groups (see Fullan, 1982, pp. 180–92).

After examining the roles and dilemmas of college coordinators in 21 court-mandated secondary school/university pairings in Boston between 1975 and 1982, a study found that coordinators had to break down a conventional view that they were in schools to hand out advice or perform needed services without sharing in activities or decision making. Hamlin's (1983) interviews revealed the uneasy path toward cooperation. One headmaster summarized the skepticism about outsiders felt by many of his colleagues: "They were a little afraid of us; we were a little afraid of them. We all wanted to make sure that we protected our own turf. And trust was a factor." Other school personnel resented any sign of external control: "They felt they knew how to do it better." Another school leader commented that the school "needed real help, not the help the Court wanted you to have." After discussions with a university coordinator, "I gave a little; she gave a little, and we worked it out together." Similarly, coordinators reported that cooperation depended on their "visibility, time, and demonstration of willingness to help" (quoted in Hamlin, 1983, pp. 139–40, 158).

When school partnerships are sustained over time through leadership support and flexible adjustments to voluntary contributions, they bring outside perspectives and expertise to a school setting. Those outsiders who have experienced the school ethos, developed a working relationship with some individuals, and assessed their potential contributions also support change as part of "ongoing program building in an organizational context" (McLaughlin and Marsh, 1978, p. 87). School leaders can both encourage outside partners and use those relationships to assess the larger social, political and economic environments.

We believe school partnerships provide ideal ways to introduce outside perspectives, expert advice, and some additional resources to school improvement processes without the conflicts and contradictory reactions that often follow from paid consultants. Because they involve interactive processes of shared benefits, teachers and outside partners can be mutually empowered through activities and through evolving understandings of their roles in social change. Loosely structured, flexible, voluntary, and innovative, partnerships invite risk taking and experimentation without threatening the core mission of affiliated institutions.

LEADERSHIP AND EMPOWERMENT

School leadership that builds partnerships is interactive and situational. It starts by supporting teaching—setting a context, organizing resources, motivating others, coordinating a rich array of activities, accepting failures as well as successes, and continually involving those left out of current activities. Investigations of secondary school partnerships with institutions of higher education verify the multiple roles and tasks of leaders in school improvement.

A study of selected Boston secondary schools during 1980–1981 suggested how a headmaster influenced the effectiveness of school-based teams. Without support and information from the administrator, teams seldom flourished. Yet when headmasters dominated the group, teacher interest soon disappeared. Communication between a team and a headmaster empowered teachers and other members of school staffs: "Team members expressed great respect for the ability of the headmaster as team leader to not only listen to all sides of a discussion, but also to push people to articulate their opinions and defend their arguments." Teachers in effective teams felt "they all had the power to make things happen for the school and they were proud of their association with the headmaster on the team" (O'Donnell, 1982, pp. 213–14).

Successful leaders overcame distrust and skepticism. In so doing, Boston school/university pairings developed capacities to " . . . handle constructively some *conflict*, absorb some *failure*, and demonstrate *growth* and *change* over time" (Hamlin, 1983, pp. 236–37). Coordinators used a variety of interpersonal strategies to overcome institutional barriers to cooperation. They recognized networks of people within schools and among organizations, adapted ideas at the local level, and involved groups in problem solving.

Their collaborative roles resembled those of earlier school managers as depicted by Tyack and Hansot (1982): "politically adept at building pro-school coalitions, willing to abandon a narrow professional ideology, and skillful in creating coordinated programs in individual schools" (p. 252). Leaders transform broad societal concerns and mandates into viable programs and activities within a school. Neither interorganizational negotiations nor individual discussions alone yield substantive change efforts. Organizational commitments do not generate a sense of involvement and ownership among most people. Individual interests lack organizational endorsement or support. Successful leaders welcome outsider participation as a way to operationalize the "obliged to" mandates of organizations into individual-based "want to" participation.

Alternatives and teams cannot flourish unless the leadership is perceived as treating them fairly—neither special rewards nor unusual burdens as compared with each other or standard programs. When collaborative projects serve students who have been systematically mistreated by society and schools, they require extra support from administrators and outside organizations. Too often leaders have overburdened those teachers most willing to tackle difficult problems. Teachers with skills and sympathy for special needs children will often find so many placed in their classroom that they become ineffective. Schools in low-income neighborhoods lack resources to overcome the burdens of poverty. Leadership has to recognize variations in educational costs and adjust resources in the direction of equal outcomes.

PROJECT ASSESSMENTS

Empowerment means sharing leadership roles and encouraging active participation in assessment activities by all those involved with collaborative projects. In order for assessments not to be defensive or self-congratulatory, small-group leaders must feel they too are being supported. Formative assessments provide valuable information when they lead to mid-course corrections. Following an action research approach, the questions asked must connect to factors within the collaborative project's control.

Examining the question of performance effectiveness in interorganizational settings, Kimberly, Norling, and Weiss (1983) observed:

(2) To the extent that there are many parties who control critical resources and have diverse orientations toward the focal organization, performance pressures will be complex and perhaps contradictory.

(3) The more complex and contradictory the performance pressures, the less satisfactory traditional measures of effectiveness are likely to be. Other criteria may have to be developed. These criteria are likely to involve informal, less visible as opposed to formal, visible aspects of how the terms and conditions of a focal organization's existence are negotiated. (p. 262)

Ordinarily, the most useful assessments are conducted by individuals or teams implementing specific school improvement projects. For instance, when Susan Savitt developed a series of workshops to help teachers in Roosevelt interact with parents, she conducted evaluations of each workshop and a needs assessment to inform the design of subsequent modules. The questions were few, direct, and pointed at specific components of the workshop. In addition, she maintained logs of participants and planning sessions so that the project's development could be viewed as a coherent response to both general and specific needs, resources, schedules, and unfolding outcomes. She audiotaped the sessions and later reflected on each presentation.

Savitt (1986) documented a straightforward approach to assessment. Each workshop for teachers included several parts with specific objectives, procedures, and evaluation questions, as in the following illustration:

OBJECTIVE 6—MODULE 2

To familiarize participants with various models of parent involvement and to assist them in ascertaining the likenesses and differences inherent in the various models.

PROCEDURE—OBJECTIVE 6—MODULE 2

(1) The workshop facilitator shared a pictorial representation of various parent involvement models with participants.

(2) Participants engaged in discussion during which the workshop facilitator encouraged them to compare and contrast the various models.

(3) Participants selected the model, based upon group consensus, which they would like to use in building parent/school interaction in their school and substantiated why they selected the particular model.

EVALUATION QUESTIONS—OBJECTIVE 6—MODULE 2

(1) Did the facilitator present the modules in a manner which was understood by participants?

(2) Were the participants able to (a) select a parent/school interaction model to use in their setting, and (b) substantiate why they selected the model? (pp. 100–101)

Teachers indicated that the models clarified their thinking. One teacher described a model as "something to work toward. It made parent/school interaction more real" (quoted in Savitt, 1986, p. 111).

At the end of five scheduled workshops, Savitt conducted a summative evaluation. Overwhelmingly, teachers described their experiences as relevant; voluntary attendance had increased at each session; and participants listed specific lessons and their intentions to apply those ideas in their interactions with parents. They volunteered comments about this staff development experience: "The rapport established by the workshop leader between herself and the teachers was based on warmth, knowledge, and true concern." Another appreciated the "home-grown" presenters: "I have gained much in self-image from realizing the quality of professionals we have here." A third summarized the case for school-based improvement projects: "We have become mired in discipline, confusion, and depression that we sometimes feel nothing else can be done." But new ideas and the enthusiasm shared with colleagues altered that belief: "We have control over making the situation better. I for one intend to do so" (quoted in Savitt, 1986, p. 163).

In completing her study, Savitt revisited the school a year later to assess longer-term effects from her workshops. Twenty-six out of 30 respondents reported that parent/school interactions had improved, and their comments suggested specifics of awareness and competence: "I have become a better listener—less apt to shoot from the hip;" and "I feel better prepared to help parents overcome their negative feelings since I have overcome mine" (quoted in Savitt, 1986, pp. 166, 171–172). Both positive and negative feedback guided the project development and informed leadership about teacher concerns and effective staff development techniques. But the real value of this extensive record of needs, activities, and assessments could be read largely between the lines—that teachers felt more competent in their roles and more pride in their district.

EVALUATING PARTNERSHIPS

All projects discussed in this book demonstrated evidence of school improvement, teacher development, and student gains. At one level, collaborative projects are relatively easy to evaluate. Because participation is voluntary, the number of people involved in activities provides a good measure of project viability. Overall, 1,000 teachers and administrators have taken courses or shared in activities of BSSP. Thousands of individuals from low-income neighborhoods participated in programs or related activities in Worcester. The Roosevelt project impacted on all grades and schools in that district. Over 100 participants in the ECS Program received Master's degrees. Admitting 25 students a year, MESTEP has assembled a network of 40 high-technology companies and school districts in eastern Massachusetts.

Projects continually assess their progress while identifying strengths and weaknesses. Ongoing evaluations provide a sense of how participants respond to joint activities. Such evidence is often anecdotal, although systematically gathered. For instance, BSSP regularly conducted formative evaluations. One teacher responded that "the program keeps her sane, it is a significant anti-boredom potion, keeps her brain going." Professor Barbara Love's course helped her development of a bibliography for a citywide workshop. Another teacher commented that the "program gives people a chance to gather, sit, think. . . . Participants at English High School have more faith in UMass than many other inservice operations . . . because there is a longtime commitment which means that the University is accepting some accountability for what happens" (quoted in Stec, 1978, Appendix C).

Most outside funding agencies require evaluative reports on collaborative projects. For example, in a study of BSSP conducted for the Massachusetts Department of Education, Lyman (1977) found that University courses and technical assistance directly influenced the design of the basic skills curriculum at English High School. She noted that five teachers who participated in a university course on Methods of Advanced French "improved their teaching methods and used a greater variety of materials." Moreover, "the chairman of the modern language department wrote and received an ESAA [Emergency School Assistance Act] minigrant to obtain audiovisual materials as a direct result of this course" (p. 9). Students praised a course on institutional research: "Through the course work offered by the University of Massachusetts, Amherst, there is now a small, but growing group of English High faculty who can conduct needs assessments, administer surveys, and do educational research and evaluation" (Lyman, 1977, p. 30).

Because school improvement projects often achieve outcomes in indirect ways, leaders must support a flexible approach and recognize accomplishments—whatever their source. Planned interventions seldom yield a specific result, such as student gains on a test following directly from a particular teaching approach. Well-defined programs concentrating on test items have demonstrated achievement score gains at the price of diminished student interest and self-responsibility. Further, collaborative programs may encourage compensatory adjustments. Thus, a principal or school district might redirect other energies toward those teachers uninvolved with a relatively well-supported partnership. In that case, comparative studies of outcomes will systematically underestimate the impact of new initiatives.

Throughout our case studies there were unexpected consequences— new elementary school playgrounds in Greenfield, communication between the county jail and the school system in Falmouth, field sites for MESTEP students in Lawrence, a new scheduling process at English High School, and so on. On the other hand, unforeseen events, such as demographic changes, revenue cuts, or political shifts, eroded many benefits from a well-constructed project in Worcester. The preponderance of unanticipated outcomes in most educational endeavors, as Michael Patton (1980) noted, "render useless standardized, quantitative measures of program outcomes while indicating that assessment must take place on a case by case, program by program basis" (p. 70).

Collaborations usually flourish around ill-structured problems, and leaders will accordingly find qualitative evaluations useful. Where schools know what they want and how to get it, they ordinarily pay for it directly. Such apparently well-structured projects are quite easily assessed through cost effectiveness studies. More commonly, multiple goals and strategies characterize school collaborations:

> If program implementation is characterized by a process of adaptation to local conditions, needs, and interests, then the methods used to study implementation must be open-ended, discovery oriented, and capable of describing developmental processes and program change. Qualitative methods are ideally suited to the task of describing program implementation. (Patton, 1980, p. 70)

Hence, assessments of collaborative school improvement projects seldom present convincing hard evidence of student achievement gains or school climate changes.

Partnerships between schools and parent/community groups, businesses, human service agencies, and institutions of higher education are almost always voluntaristic, and they are small compared to the home organizations. They are adaptive in their development and inherently untidy in their organizational strategies and structures. These features are real strengths of cooperative projects. Because collaborations can be arranged in a flexible manner, people and organizations accomplish change without a need to redesign or rearrange entire systems. That flexibility, however, makes it difficult to determine with certainty whether a specific program has produced an intended result.

Leaders must use appropriate assessments and understand their limitations especially for social programs with many "moving parts" and that involve "a number of circumstances in addition to those introduced by a program." Programs designed to improve equitable outcomes ordinarily have "small impacts on the social world," although they may influence some individuals profoundly. "More often than not, we can expect effects to be small and difficult to detect" (Rossi and Freeman, 1982, p. 167). Leaders can build needed support for program efforts and identify strengths and weaknesses of projects. Evaluations can recognize the useful contributions of team efforts. Summative studies help connect specific activities to larger educational visions.

LESSONS ABOUT COLLABORATION

Leaders must adopt flexible and potentially high-risk management styles and procedures if partnerships are to enable those involved to reframe improvement issues. Leaders must assure that collaborative structures remain flexible and loosely coupled. They must encourage voluntary participation (human resources frame), "personalized" networks (new structures), and special arrangements for small numbers of individuals in each cooperating organization (redistribution of power). They must value "deviant" ideas and actors, listen to suggestions and criticisms, and support experimentation (new heroes and symbols).

First, to thrive as a substructure without upsetting basic organizational patterns, partnerships can seldom be large enough to affect all members of the cooperating organizations. Although leaders endeavor to spread ideas and practices from those most directly involved to others, such directives from the top or mandates for a particular approach contradict a need for staff to "buy in" and adapt ideas to serve their particular building's needs and culture. Leaders must continually find ways to provide many people with opportunities to shape the course and direction of change through small groups and multiple approaches.

Second, most participants in partnerships attach particular importance to initial joint activities as a time of legitimate testing of expectations. Accordingly, during the beginnings of partnerships, people experience heightened tensions, periods of intense preparation and learning, and considerable anxiety about how to communicate a sense of process without reducing matters to a series of preprogrammed steps. For educational leaders within their school settings, it is a time of ascertaining expectations and standards without revealing their fears. At both personal and organizational levels, there has to be some openness about shortcomings: otherwise why would partners agree to work toward better schools? But perceived problems should be reframed as opportunities for working together in new ways.

Third, the key interests and motivations of participants are situational and contingent. Since most collaborations cannot be planned or conducted by one or two people, leaders must recognize that the assumptions and ideas of participants form a complex array of somewhat related perspectives that influence collaborative dramas. To promote cooperation, leaders must understand how all viewpoints and interests (including their own) affect the scripts and scenarios of partnerships. Whether conflict or cooperation ensues often depends on a leader's ability to acknowledge weaknesses and emphasize mutual payoffs.

Fourth, leaders should realize that they cannot behave as "outsiders" to processes of collaboration in which they are immersed. At the earliest stages, leaders must openly identify their personal goals, commitments, and potential contributions while inviting other participants to do the same. Also, leaders in both organizations should clarify some boundaries and off-limit areas in order to suggest realistic expectations. A lack of clear statements by partners, particularly during the initial stages, engenders conflicts arising from unstated differences, unrecognized cross-purposes, and diverging interests.

At the same time, leaders must recognize that some aspects of collaborative projects should remain undefined. Weick (1979) argued that ambiguity was mostly negative when it surrounded group procedures and agendas, but useful when applied to matters of short-term/long-term goals and objectives. A partnership can assign responsibility for specific activities while leaving means and ends unplanned. Leaders must orchestrate a balance between clarity and vagueness in project planning and development.

Fifth, from the perspectives of key players in both organizations, there ordinarily exists a continual need to express support and satisfaction with the collaboration. They typically recount a particular incident to demonstrate some success, although that outcome may be only tangentially related to the partnership. This behavior may also reflect a belief that announcing successes produces positive public relations. Because self-praise seldom spurs improvements, leaders must balance this positive tone with a recognition of unmet challenges and changing institutional needs.

Many ill-structured problems reflect symptoms of other issues that may be intractable from the standpoint of a classroom, a school, a district, or a collaboration. Hence, leaders should encourage collaborative partners to support shared activities in a belief that much will be learned by trying to change organizational patterns. Leaders must avoid situations where an approach that was successful in one situation becomes the ready solution in other contexts. Sometimes a variety of alternatives encourages participation and postpones determining a new organizational pattern.

Sixth, the shaping of a shared reality is never easy—particularly with successes. Failures are more predictable, in part because they fit a pattern of frustrations about others who do not view the world and its issues in a "proper" context. Most collaborations are surrounded by interested spectators in both organizations who decided against participation, and they usually welcome evidence of breakdown and failure. Such a Greek chorus often fosters an "us against them" attitude among those most active in a collaborative substructure. Those suspicions can further accentuate the severity of conflicting views about the purposes and outcomes of collaboration that ordinarily develop among insiders and outsiders.

As partnerships develop, they will require new management and leadership approaches. They may start with resources for doing more of the same, but they cannot end there. They may begin with shared activities and diverse ends, but they should then foster communication that promotes some shared goals and some diverse means. They open with teachers in traditional roles but must gradually build enthusiasm and empower a new professionalism. They must allow new understandings and dynamics to unlock possibilities and foster new strategies and structures.

Ideally, leaders can use collaborations to foster institutional responses to rapidly changing conditions by serving as a "scouting party," or a research and development center for schools. If they evolve, they change purposes and activities. Often they experience a turnover of staff and of key supporters. Collaborative leaders address ill-structured problems by rearranging existing personnel and resources to modify organizational practices within a loosely coupled educational system. Their evolving understandings of schooling and society then transform both collaborative activities and purposes into school improvements.

10

Educational Purposes
and Future Societies

Throughout this study, we have described collaborative activities in terms of multiple realities, ill-structured problems, and reflexivity in order to illustrate how to think about school improvement partnerships. Professional and organizational developments depend on the time, place, and personalities of participants as well as scenarios of interaction among individuals. Each partnership has its own history, and its experiences have different meanings for each participant or observer. These diverse accounts involve common processes of interaction, but no blueprint for initiating, implementing and assessing collaborative projects. Furthermore, as partnerships develop or unravel, resolutions continually give way to new problems and agreements.

Although shaped by the circumstances and personalities of a particular project, most collaborative experiences have been encountered by others in different guises. For example, building trust and initiating connecting activities among members of two organizations are predictable hurdles, but each project must find its own way to establish communication networks, to build a sense of win-win possibilities, and to sustain occasions for mutually beneficial interchanges. Although partners must improvise in order to support linkages and identify potential benefits, they can directly observe whether their activities and understandings lead to new strategies and structures that empower teachers and schools.

We have recommended partnerships as a means to create possibilities for education so that future societies may hold greater choices. Change in teachers, schools and future societies is unlikely if collaborations merely facilitate low-cost, short-term offers of materials or volunteered services. School partnerships will develop little of their potential unless they engage teachers as active decision makers both in their classrooms and in devising a comprehensive school curriculum; help schools and their larger communities agree on goals, standards, and implementation plans; and stimulate discussions among insiders and outsiders over educational purposes related to both equality and quality.

SCHOOLS AND FUTURE SOCIETIES

Nearly one in four Americans currently attends school at some level from prekindergarten through advanced graduate study. What they do and learn through schooling affects how organizations are structured, America's social choices and values, and the future of a planet that seems ever more interdependent. Teachers have developed curriculum and tested their students in ways that support competition and individualism. Will they also model cooperation and group processes? Many Americans continue to assume that knowledge is good, and therefore technological frontiers should be explored. That rationale has supported heart transplants but not regular aerobic exercise and promoted military research for complex weapons but not studies of organic farming. Will schools in the future emphasize aesthetic expression and moral values rather than technocratic and material solutions? The underlying directions are of transcendent importance.

If partnerships are to work effectively with schools, outsiders will have to acknowledge both the endemic dilemmas and the valuable experiences of teachers, who are preparing children to function in an information-rich service economy. By clarifying the key services performed by schools, members of other organizations may come to understand their shared interests and competing roles with teachers and schools. Potential partners can initiate useful discussions about organizational strengths and weaknesses—as well as current needs and future goals. That dialogue should start with common concerns rather than pointing a finger of blame.

First, school partners share an interest in ascertaining what skills, competencies, and experiences will prepare today's youth for life in the twenty-first century. Although shaped by past decisions, the answer is open-ended and subject to choice as well as chance. Certainly schools strongly influence American attitudes about cultural diversity, ecology, peace, and international relations. Because schools involve such massive commitments of time and funds, they invite reflection over ways to foster a better society. At the same time, individual classrooms, instructional programs, and school climate can be affected through a few extra resources and volunteered time that foster interactive group processes among staff and outsiders.

Second, teachers share characteristics with many other service employees. As educated professionals, they determine the quality of their work by delivering services through interactions with others. Increasingly, large organizations employ many workers to support other subunits of the firm. Executives have tried to assure coordination of workers and units through informal quota systems, intra-organizational profit centers, and new layers of managers and committees; however, cooperation ultimately depends on the staff's pride in quality workmanship and their loyalty to the firm's goals. Effective school leaders have built consensus around shared goals and high expectations, and those lessons may serve other organizations. Coordination of workers with essential knowledge or skills resembles good staff development practices in schools more than it does traditional factory supervision.

Third, new information is a fascinating product of growing importance to all kinds of enterprises, and schools are microcosms of information-saturated societies. Teachers connect complex scientific and cultural knowledge with a background in child development. No one person in an organization can know everything necessary for that planning and decision making, but schools provide a useful model for organizing facts and theories and maintaining their accessibility. Among staff and students, there is a wealth of knowledge about each student and the instructional repertoires of teachers that can be drawn on as desired. Hence, organizations increasingly create structures and processes for linking knowledge-holders and decision makers.

Finally, educators continually wrestle with the connections between knowledge and an individual's or organization's capacity to act purposefully. Direct, specific prescriptions may prepare students to complete forms; workers to perform useful tasks; and citizens to pay income taxes. But schooling also should prepare adults for uncertainty, ambiguity, group processes, and the forming of one's personal and social values. Critical thinking must continually balance competing purposes and values—asking how individual freedoms and responsibilities can fit with those of others and considering how organizational structures and decision-making rules affect individual perceptions and powers. New possibilities arise both from disciplined inquiry and from grappling with ill-structured problems that hold a dream of a better world.

LEARNING FROM SCHOOLS

Partnerships facilitate a two-way transfer of perspectives and processes, and outside organizations can build on many demonstrations of school-based ideas and programs. Parent and community organizations have often benefited from sessions about child-raising, about leisure time activities, or about community concerns such as drug abuse or sex education. They learn most when local teachers and community members are involved in hands-on activities, role playing, and practical projects that build group processes. Furthermore, museums, libraries, theater groups, and recreational leagues can utilize instructional practices and share media resources with schools in ways that redefine community education (Reed and Loughran, 1984).

Businesses increasingly conduct staff training in formal settings. Corporations have hired teachers and staff developers for instructional techniques and experience in constructing a curriculum for adult learners. Firms have recognized the value of a long-term investment in on-the-job training of their employees, and some have established counseling and mental health services to rehabilitate workers who have experienced job-related stress or illnesses such as alcoholism. Businesses have added athletic fields and exercise facilities as part of their employment benefits so that some plants look like a collegiate campus—while many high schools still resemble a nineteenth-century factory. Through work-release programs and creative partnerships, many firms are strengthening the connection between career training and marketable skills.

Business leaders have also discovered that their involvement with schools has reshaped their sense of social responsibility. As a result of American Can Company's partnership with the Martin Luther King School in Manhattan, its president has become an outspoken advocate of increased funding for schools. In a revealing interview, William Woodside (1986) indicated how small involvements had grown: "When we took over as a partner there, it had the lowest after-school activity rate of any high school in New York City. Today, it has by far the highest." American Can supported extra compensation for teachers' overtime, but Woodside also lobbied in Albany and Washington for higher salaries and modern equipment.

Significantly, Woodside (1986) related the case for school finance reforms to a broad vision of society—especially to the reduction of poverty as an ethical value.

But I also try to take it out of such a long-term vista by talking about the loss of an effective work force. As business gets more and more complicated, we're producing students who can do fewer and fewer complicated things. Right now, business spends more on education and training than all the private school systems do.

The other thing I talk about is that education is one of the first steps toward making an adequate income. If you're surrounded by a world where most of the incomes are inadequate, how do you expect to survive as a corporation and sell your products?

Through a partnership, this business executive both perceived and articulated the interdependence of modern society.

Human service agencies have often hired teachers for their staff, and they have recognized that instruction and prevention are as important to their function as therapeutic counseling. Further, many agencies have established close, informal relationships with school staffs so that information, requests for assistance, and encouragement are exchanged several times a week in response to problems of individual students and their families. For example, a neighborhood center in Worcester has cooperated with nearby schools, especially the Grafton Street Elementary School. With a gymnasium and facilities for serving meals, Friendly House has provided athletic training and a location for graduations and celebratory dinners. In turn, the school has accommodated children in families being sheltered at Friendly House. Both organizations insist that the social and physical well-being of students and their families is important for academic success.

No organization has more to learn from schools than institutions of higher education, although a perceived hierarchy has raised barriers to those lessons. Presumably new knowledge is disseminated from advanced research universities down to kindergartens. During the early years of this century, when organized knowledge grew rapidly in higher education as new departmental structures and professional academic roles focused on research and publication, such a model for information dissemination was fairly realistic. High schools grew as enrollments expanded, and many teachers were neither well-trained nor encouraged to keep up with their discipline. Salaries and prestige have gone to research and advanced study—although researchers have demonstrated that the important years of learning for individuals occur before the age of five.

Currently, elementary and secondary teachers are well-prepared professionals who are frustrated by their inability to apply what they know (McNeil, 1986). Higher education might well help teachers and other educators to use and disseminate available knowledge. Alternative learning and teaching styles might recognize adult competencies that have great social consequence but little place in the formal curriculum of elite institutions. Researchers might investigate what kinds of settings and prospects would improve education and jobs for poor and minority students. Although American historians have expanded their coverage of Black history, as well as contributions by women, families and laborers, most teacher preparation programs still ignore Asian, African, and Hispanic cultures and their relevance for children in today's world.

Perhaps the most important contribution of schooling to higher education over the past decade has followed from efforts to understand why schools resist change. Studies of school cultures, effective schools, and work lives of teachers have strengthened a picture of organizational development and outcomes that is far less behavioral and mechanistic than earlier research studies. Although incomplete, ethnographic studies have described school climates in ways that facilitate a broad understanding of current dilemmas (see Graubard, 1981a, 1981b). They have influenced thinking about educational reforms with their emphases on improving professionalism for all teachers.

PURPOSES AND EQUITABLE OUTCOMES

Reform proposals have raised both hopes and frustrations over the past two decades, but the key point is that school improvement is not one solution to a single problem. It requires more than a comprehensive response to multiple issues. School reform requires many initiatives and active involvement by all interested parties. Change will occur in each school as professional staff become engaged in reconsidering their purposes. Those discussions are eased by a social climate that welcomes that debate with its potential for raising divisive issues as well as discovering shared beliefs. A team of experienced educational reformers has stressed that "as long as we care about schools they will touch our deepest emotions about ourselves, our children, our past, and our future" (Lazerson, McLaughlin, McPherson, and Bailey, 1986, p. xiii).

After reviewing collaborative experiences of teachers and school leaders, we concluded that participants had gained important insights into their role in society. Working in groups on specific projects to improve their own schools, they had presented themselves to others in new ways, tested different visions of reality, addressed deeper issues of education, and learned about themselves and their setting. Broad goals and shared activities linked teachers with outside partners in a national movement for educational reform. Even as they faced possible retrenchment, Worcester teachers spoke of "a banding together of dedicated professionals to guarantee the survival of the teacher profession and the public school" (Belevick and Little-Porter, 1982). Partnerships open doors for teachers and citizens to re-engage in discussions that recognize the public interest in equity as well as efficiency.

Throughout this century, narrow professional control, embodied in an emphasis on one best system, attempted to wall out community pressures and to limit school committees to policy-setting roles. As a result, schools responded to political pressures in an indirect fashion: that is, they heeded organized groups and business interests with proposals and solutions that enhanced roles for educators (Tyack, 1974). That outcome was tolerable during a rapid expansion of secondary-school enrollments and economic shifts that increasingly rewarded post-secondary study. Although schools were still segregated, unequal, and unresponsive to children with special needs, they also became better and fairer in distinctly measurable ways during the 1950s and 1960s. Rapidly expanding enrollments temporarily muted protests from those who were educationally cheated.

Paradoxically, as schools achieved mass education at the secondary level, applied new technologies to both instruction and management, and reduced glaring inequities against minorities, females, students with special needs, and others, their remaining failures appeared more frustrating. As de jure segregation disappeared, de facto segregation in metropolitan areas between central cities and suburbs increased racial isolation in schools and maintained a pattern of distinctly lower resources for predominantly low-income and minority districts. Alternative programs have engaged many students in humane and exciting learning communities, while other alternatives have allowed some students to put in time without instruction or standards.

Successfully promoting an individualistic, high-growth, materialistic, and technological society, schools transformed American life and generated demands for reforms and a new mission. Based on current trends, by the end of the 1980s the United States will have more professional, managerial and technical workers than the total of skilled, semiskilled and unskilled blue-collar workers. In 1986, wholesale and retail trades employed some 24 million, the service sector over 23 million, and manufacturing just over 19 million—nearly 2 million less than at the beginning of the decade. As an expert in labor statistics has noted, professional, managerial and technical workers have little in common except "the requirement for education and training, often life-long interest in a discipline, a broader latitude for creativity, independent thought and action, career advancement potential and opportunities for greater recognition" (Ehrenhalt, 1986).

Because schools are complex, multifaceted organizations with professional staffs and the energy of millions of students, any discussion about purposes should start with basic principles in order to focus the debate. Roosevelt staff described an ideal teacher as a caring and humane person who could respond not only to individual needs, but also to the harm caused by racism and class bias. Then the staff examined the school setting in light of equity, efficiency, and choice. Similar goals have commonly been related to the nature of American society:

Schools must be both equal and excellent. Equality in education is predicated on the belief that in a democracy all citizens are entitled to the skills necessary for thoughtful and active citizenship. Excellence in education comes from a commitment to learning, ranging from the basic skills of literacy and problem solving, to creative and critical thinking, to the desire to expand still further one's knowledge and skills. (Lazerson, McLaughlin, McPherson, and Bailey, 1986, p. xiii)

Despite many efforts to express an academic agenda without describing the setting and students, these catchwords of equity, efficiency, and excellence take on their significance from the unexpressed assumptions about what kind of future lies ahead. If nuclear war is probable, then basic survival skills combined with a curriculum emphasizing international relations and disarmament would take priority over liberal arts or computers. If emerging business firms are less hierarchical and more dependent on professional expertise, then schools should incorporate both more independent work and more cooperative projects. If the major challenge is domestic cohesion, then schools might emphasize American history and culture. If the United States must adapt to a world of many nations, then a multicultural approach will pay large dividends.

But none of these issues will mean much if school responses continue to reinforce existing patterns of social hierarchy and discrimination. Only if schools offer a meaningful equality of opportunity will they gain support and cooperation from currently excluded groups. The possibility of inclusion in powerful institutions and groups is essential to motivate students to learn and to prepare for future employment. "The problem of power is thus critical to the effective behavior of people in organizations," Rosabeth M. Kanter (1977) concluded. "Power issues occupy center stage not because individuals are greedy for more, but because some people are incapacitated without it" (p. 205).

As the world has become more urbanized and richer in goods and services, the quality of life is increasingly affected by what others do and by our surrounding communities. Previous localisms and inequities in schools become increasingly intolerable. More and more activities involve a mixture of public and private support and regulations. As long as some large organizations exist, individuals will need to connect with institutional support in order to influence policies by those large bodies. Otherwise, isolated individuals will increasingly feel powerless in determining their own futures. Only those persons who have access to organizational control will be able to shape their personal and social development.

In Albert O. Hirschman's (1970) terms, these conditions mean greater emphasis on voice and less on exit as a response to declining organizations. That voice—from workers, members or broader public groups— would be enhanced if it incorporated organizational as well as individual perspectives. Open discussions among partners or working groups can bring multiple realities and solutions into the picture as a way jointly to reframe possibilities. Because organizations not only repeat patterns of behavior but also learn from their successes and failures, society benefits from having existing groups adopt and adapt new approaches rather than continually replacing one structure with another.

Although issues of planning future societies seem somewhat removed from school partnerships, no one can discuss school improvements without including many implications about human nature and the kind of society one would like to see. However vague and diffuse, these debates will continue as central forces affecting schools and the professional lives of teachers. These negotiations are necessarily tentative and open-ended since no one group or organization controls future options. Nevertheless, a group consensus about certain values affects behaviors and outcomes; for example, effective schools convey both standards and expectations to students and teachers based on an implicit vision of a future community. Partnerships cannot directly create those future societies, but they can foster interactive planning based on authentic and varied voices that may shape agreements around win-win exchanges.

Within organizations, the case for greater equality and access is fairly clear in the context of innovations. Changes that augment the resources or authority of those already in power ordinarily encourage a negative reaction among those who lack influence and sooner or later a stalemate emerges. Such changes seldom add capacity to the total organization, and they discourage new ideas and resources. If both absolute power and the absence of power are corrupting, the goals would seem to be involvement, voice for all, and active participation. Authority should relate to responsibilities and to performance in ways that enhance the capacity of every member of an organization. Preparation for those new patterns can start with teachers and students in schools.

Many school partners have established their credentials as knowledgeable and serious discussants of educational weaknesses and strengths, and their help and support will be greatly needed to establish agreement on both purposes and approaches to school improvement. Shared activities with outside partners will raise troublesome issues and require mutual accommodation, but the promise of new insights and unanticipated outcomes is also real and compelling. Teachers may explore new definitions of professionalism and shape evolving strategies and structures of schools. Students and parents may discover a new sense of educational purpose and a vision of a better future.

Bibliography

American Council of Life Insurance. (n.d. [1983]). *Company-school collaboration, A manual for developing successful projects.* Washington, DC: Author.

Axelrod, R. (1984). *The evolution of cooperation.* New York: Basic Books.

Barton, P. E. (1983). *Partnerships between corporations and schools* (Research Report Series). Washington, DC: National Commission for Employment Policy.

Barth, R. S. (1980). *Run school run.* Cambridge: Harvard University Press.

Belevick, E., and Little-Porter, M. E. (1982). *Where do we go from here?* Unpublished manuscript.

Bellah, R., Madsen, R., Sullivan, W., Swidler, A., and Tipton, S. (1985). *Habits of the heart: Individualism and commitment in American life.* New York: Harper and Row.

Berger, P. L., and Luckmann, T. (1967). *The social construction of reality.* Garden City, NY: Doubleday Anchor.

Berman, P. (1981). Educational change: An implementation paradigm. In R. Lehming and M. Kane (eds.), *Improving schools: Using what we know* (pp. 253–86). Beverly Hills, CA: Sage Publications.

Berman, P., and McLaughlin, M. (1978). *Federal programs supporting eduational change, Vol. VII: Factors affecting implementation and continuation.* Santa Monica, CA: Rand Corporation.

Blumberg, A., and Greenfield, W. (1986). *The effective principal* (2d ed.). Boston: Allyn and Bacon.

Bolman, L. G., and Deal, T. E. (1984). *Modern approaches to understanding and managing organizations.* San Francisco: Jossey-Bass.

Boyer, E. (1983). *High school: A report on secondary education in America.* New York: Harper and Row.

Bratiotis, D. (1982). Implications of teacher coping strategies for staff development in urban middle schools. Ed.D. diss., University of Massachusetts at Amherst.

Bremer, J., and Von Moschzisker, M. (1971). *The school without walls.* New York: Holt, Rinehart and Winston.

Bronfenbrenner, U. (1979). *The ecology of human development*. Cambridge: Harvard University Press.

Caldwell, B. M. (February, 1986). Day care and the public schools—natural allies, natural enemies. *Educational Leadership*, pp. 34–39.

Campbell, S. E. (1984). [Conclusions and suggestions based on team interviews, Boston Secondary Schools Project]. Unpublished raw data.

Carew, J., and Lightfoot, S. L. (1979). *Beyond bias: Perspectives on classrooms*. Cambridge: Harvard University Press.

Cetron, M. (1985). *Schools of the future*. New York: McGraw-Hill.

Clark, R. J. (1982). [December Boston Secondary Schools Project Participant Feedback]. Unpublished raw data.

Clark, R. J., Johnson, R., Kessler, R., and Schultz, K. (1984). Solving the math and science teacher shortage: One district's initiative. *Spectrum*, 2(2), 31–35.

Cohen, M. (October 5, 1985). After 10 years, pairing of Boston schools, area colleges is hailed as national model. *Boston Globe*, p. 23.

College Board. (1984). *Academic preparation for college: What students need to know and be able to do*. New York: Author.

Comer, J. P. (1980). *School power: Implications of an intervention project*. New York: Free Press.

Committee For Economic Development/Research and Policy Committee. (1985). *Investing in our children*. New York: Author.

Darling-Hammond, L. (1984). *Beyond the commission reports*. Santa Monica, CA: Rand Corporation.

Davies, D. (1978). It can be done. In P. Collins (ed.), *Teacher Corps national conference report 1978*. (Contract No. 300–77–0156, pp. 80–83). Washington, DC: Teacher Corps.

Deal, T. E. (1986). Educational change: Revival tent, tinkertoys, jungle, or carnival. In A. Lieberman (ed.), *Rethinking school improvement* (pp. 115–28). New York: Teachers College Press.

———. (1987). The culture of schools. In L. T. Sheive and M. B. Schoenheit (eds.), *Leadership: Examining the elusive* (pp. 3–15). Alexandria, VA: Association for Supervision and Curriculum Development.

Deal, T. E., and Kennedy, A. A. (1982). *Corporate cultures*. Reading, MA: Addison-Wesley.

De Bevoise, W. (February 1986). Collaboration: Some principles of bridgework. *Educational Leadership*, pp. 9–12.

Dennison, G. (1969). *The lives of children*. New York: Random House.

Dillon-Peterson, B. (ed.). (1981). *Staff development/organization development*. Alexandria, VA: Association for Supervision and Curriculum Development.

Douglas, J. D. (1974). *Defining America's social problems*. Englewood Cliffs, NJ: Prentice-Hall.

Durkin, J. E. (1975). Mini-sabbatical: An alternative model of staff development for urban schools. Ed.D. diss., University of Massachusetts at Amherst.

Edmonds, R. (December 1982). Programs of school improvement: An overview. *Educational Leadership*, pp. 4–11.

Edmonds, R., and Frederiksen, J. (1978). *Search for effective schools: The identification and analysis of schools that are instructionally effective for poor children.* Cambridge: Harvard University Center for Urban Studies.

Ehrenhalt, S. M. (August 15, 1986). Economic scene: Work-force shifts in 80's. *New York Times*, p. D–2.

Emery, C. A., and Jones, B. L. (June 1980). Achievements of a planning year. *New England Teacher Corps Exchange*, pp. 6–7.

———. (July, 1982). Final report: UMass/Worcester staff development project, 1979–1982 (Processes/Practices/Products No. 35). Amherst, MA: University of Massachusetts, School of Education.

Eurich, N. (1985). *Corporate classrooms: The learning business.* Princeton, NJ: Carnegie Foundation for the Advancement of Teaching.

Fetterman, D. M. (1984). Ethnography in educational research. In D. M. Fetterman (ed.), *Ethnography in educational evaluation* (pp. 21–35). Beverly Hills, CA: Sage Publications.

Filmer, P., Phillipson, M., Silverman, D., and Walsh, D. (1972). *New directions in sociological theory.* Cambridge: MIT Press.

Fingarette, H. (1963). *The self in transformation.* New York: Harper and Row.

Fraser, L. A. (1985–1986). The Atlanta adopt-a-school program: Innovative interactions. *Action in Teacher Education*, 7(4), 17–22.

Friedman, J. (1973). *Retracking America: A theory of transactive planning.* New York: Anchor Press.

Fullan, M. (1982). *The meaning of educational change.* New York: Teachers College Press.

Garfinkel, H. (1967). *Studies in ethnomethodology.* Englewood Cliffs, NJ: Prentice-Hall.

Geertz, C. (1973). *The interpretation of culture.* New York: Basic Books.

Gentry, A., Jones, B., Peelle, C., Phillips, R., Woodbury J., and Woodbury, R. (1972). *Urban education: The hope factor.* Philadelphia: Saunders.

Gilligan, C. F. (1977). In a different voice: Women's conceptions of self and of morality. *Harvard Educational Review*, 47(4), 481–517.

———. (1982). *In a different voice: Psychological theory and women's development.* Cambridge: Harvard University Press.

Gittell, M. (1980). *Limits to citizen participation: The decline of community organizations.* Beverly Hills, CA: Sage Publications.

Goodlad, J. (1975). *The dynamics of educational change.* New York: McGraw-Hill.

———. (1984). *A place called school.* New York: McGraw-Hill.

Graubard, S. R. (ed.). (1981a). America's schools: Public and private [Special Issue]. *Daedalus*, 110(3).

———. (1981b). America's schools: Portraits and perspectives [Special Issue]. *Daedalus*, 110(4).

Hamlin, B. R. (1983). The campus coordinator's role as technical assistant to the principal/headmaster in Boston pairings 1975–1982. Ed.D. diss., University of Massachusetts at Amherst.

Heck, S. F. and Williams, C. R. (1984). *The complex roles of the teacher.* New York: Teachers College Press.

Henderson, A. (ed.). (1981). *Parent participation—student achievement: The evidence grows.* Columbia, MD: National Committee for Citizens in Education.

Hirschman, A. O. (1970). *Exit, voice, and loyalty: Responses to decline in firms, organizations, and states.* Cambridge: Harvard University Press.

Jackson, P. (1968). *Life in classrooms.* New York: Holt, Rinehart and Winston.

Jencks, C., Smith, M., Acland, H., Bane, M. J., Cohen, D., Gintis, H., Heyns, B., and Michelson, S. (1972). *Inequality: A reassessment of the effect of family and schooling in America.* New York: Basic Books.

Jones, B. L. (1982). [Unpublished lecture notes].

Jones, B. L., comp. (January 1983). A report on Roosevelt Public Schools: Strengths and potential improvements. University of Massachusetts at Amherst.

Jones, B. L., and Maloy, R. W. (1986). Collaboration and ill-structured problems of school improvement. *Planning & Changing, 17*(1), 3–8.

Joyce, B. R. (1981). Making the strange familiar: Scenes from a future teacher's life. In B. Dillon-Peterson (ed.), *Staff development/organizational development* (pp. 128–35). Alexandria, VA: Association for Supervision and Curriculum Development.

Joyce, B. R., Hersh, R. H. and McKibbin, M. (1983). *The structure of school improvement.* New York: Longman.

Kanter, R. M. (1977). *Men and women of the corporation.* New York: Basic Books.

Katz, M. B. (1971). *Class, bureaucracy, and schools: The illusion of educational change in America.* New York: Praeger.

Kegan, R. (1982). *The evolving self: Problem and process in human development.* Cambridge: Harvard University Press.

Kegan, R., and Lahey, L. (1984). Adult leadership and adult development: A constructivist view. In B. Kellerman (ed.), *Leadership: Multidisciplinary perspectives* (pp. 199–230). Englewood, NJ: Prentice-Hall.

Kimberly, J. R., Norling, F., and Weiss, J. A. (1983). Pondering the performance puzzle: Effectiveness in interorganizational settings. In R. H. Hall and R. E. Quinn (eds.), *Organizational theory and public policy* (pp. 249–64). Beverly Hills, CA: Sage Publications.

Kirst, M. (1984). *Who controls our schools?* New York: W. H. Freeman.

Knowles, M. (1978). *The adult learner: A neglected species.* Houston, TX: Gulf Publishing.

Lazerson, M., McLaughlin, J. B., McPherson, B. and Bailey, S. K. (1986). *An education of value: The purposes and practices of schools.* New York: Cambridge University Press.

Leacock, E. (1969). *Teaching and learning in city schools.* New York: Basic Books.

Lehming, R., and Kane, M. (eds.). (1981). *Improving schools: Using what we know.* Beverly Hills, CA: Sage Publications.

Lewontin, R. C., Rose, S., and Kamin, L. J. (1984). *Not in our genes: Biology, ideology, and human nature.* New York: Pantheon Books.

Lieberman, A., and Miller, L. (1984). *Teachers, their world and their work: Implications for school improvement.* Alexandria, VA: Association for Supervision and Curriculum Development.

Lieberman, A., and Miller, L. (eds.). (1979). *Staff development: New demands, new realities, new perspectives.* New York: Teachers College Press.

Lightfoot, S. L. (1978). *Worlds apart: Relationships between families and schools*. New York: Basic Books.

———. (1983). *The good high school*. New York: Basic Books.

Lipsky, M. (1980). *Street-level bureaucracy: Dilemmas of the individual in public services*. New York: Basic Books.

Lombana, J. H. (1983). *Home-school partnerships*. New York: Grune and Stratton.

Lortie, D. C. (1975). *Schoolteacher: A sociological study*. Chicago: University of Chicago Press.

Lyman, K. (1977). Evaluation report: English High School/University of Massachusetts, Amherst collaboration funded under Chapter 636. (Available from the Boston Secondary Schools Project, School of Education, University of Massachusetts at Amherst).

McHugh, P. (1968). *Defining the situation*. Indianapolis, IN: Bobbs-Merrill.

McLaughlin, M. W., and Marsh, D. D. (1978). Staff development and school change. *Teachers College Record, 80*(1), 69–94.

McNeil, L. M. (1986). *Contradictions of control: School structure and social knowledge*. New York: Routledge and Kegan Paul.

McNett, I. E. (1982). *Let's not reinvent the wheel: Profiles of school/business collaboration*. Washington, DC: Institute for Educational Leadership.

Madaus, G. F., Airasian, P. W., and Kellaghan, T. (1980). *School effectiveness: A reassessment of the evidence*. New York: McGraw-Hill.

Maeroff, G. (1983). *School and college: Partnerships in education*. Princeton, NJ: Carnegie Foundation for the Advancement of Teaching.

Maloy, R. W. (1985). The multiple realities of school-university collaboration. *The Educational Forum, 49*(3), 341–50.

Maloy, R. W. and Fischetti, J. (1985). The work of school improvement teams: A qualitative perspective. *Educational Horizons, 63*(4), 164–68.

Maloy, R. W., and Jones, B. L. (1987). Teachers, partnerships, and school improvement. *Journal of Research and Development in Education, 20*(2), 19–24.

Maloy, R. W. and Seldin, C. A. (1984). The mini-sabbatical: Connecting the off-campus graduate student to the university campus. *Continuum, 48*(2), 115–20.

Mann, D. (1984). It's up to you to steer those school/business partnerships. *The American School Board Journal, 120*(10), 20–24.

Meyer, J. (1978). The effects of education as an institution. *American Journal of Sociology, 83*(1), 55–77.

Miller, L., and Wolf, T. E. (1978). Staff development for school change: Theory and practice. In A. Lieberman and L. Miller (eds.), *Staff development: New demands, new realities, new perspectives* (pp. 144–60). New York: Teachers College Press.

Mitroff, I. I. (1983). Beyond experimentation: New methods for a new age. In E. Seidman (ed.), *Handbook of social intervention* (pp. 163–77). Beverly Hills, CA: Sage Publications.

National Commission on Excellence in Education. (1983). *A nation at risk: The imperative of educational reform*. Washington, DC: U.S. Government Printing Office.

National Science Board Commission on Precollege Education in Mathematics,

Science and Technology. (1983). *Educating Americans for the 21st century.* Washington, DC: Author.

O'Donnell, G. A. (1982). Factors affecting a staff development team approach for secondary school improvement. Ed.D. diss., University of Massachusetts at Amherst.

Olson, L. (January 15, 1986). Effective schools. *Education Week*, pp. 11–21.

———. (April 8, 1987). Network for renewal: Goodlad seeks stronger school-university alliances. *Education Week*, pp. 1, 5–6.

O'Malley, K. P. (1979). The growth and development of the Urban Studies Center: A Boston Public School alternative program of the English High School, 1971–1977. Ed.D. diss., University of Massachusetts at Amherst.

Paley, V. G. (1981). *Wally's stories.* Cambridge, MA: Harvard University Press.

Passow, A. H. (1986). Beyond the commission reports: Toward meaningful school improvement. In A. Lieberman (ed.), *Rethinking school improvement* (pp. 206–18). New York: Teachers College Press.

Patterson, J. L., Purkey, S. C., and Parker, J. V. (1986). *Productive school systems for a nonrational world.* Alexandria, VA: Association for Supervision and Curriculum Development.

Patton, M. Q. (1980). *Qualitative evaluation methods.* Beverly Hills, CA: Sage Publications.

Peelle, C. (February 1975). A new design for higher education: The UMass Center for Urban Education. *Phi Delta Kappan*, pp. 399–402.

———. (January 1977). UMass update: More smoke than fire? *Phi Delta Kappan*, pp. 439–40.

Pelletz, L. (1979). [UMass/Worcester Teacher Corps]. Unpublished raw data.

Peterkin, R. (1981). Choice in public high schools: Options as a management strategy for large urban high schools. Ed.D. diss., University of Massachusetts at Amherst.

Peters, T. J. and Waterman, R. H. (1982). *In search of excellence: Lessons from America's best-run companies.* New York: Harper and Row.

Phi Delta Kappa. (1974). *School climate improvement: A challenge to the school administrator.* Bloomington, IN: Author.

———. (1985). *School and business partnerships.* Bloomington, IN: Author.

Piaget, J. (1965). *The moral judgment of the child.* New York: Free Press. (Original work published 1932).

———. (1968). *Six psychological studies.* New York: Viking Books.

Pollner, M. (1974). Mundane reasoning. *Philosophy of the Social Sciences*, 4(1), 35–54.

Purkey, S. C., and Smith, M. S. (1983). Effective schools: A review. *The Elementary School Journal*, 83(4), 427–52.

Raphael, R. (1985). *The teacher's voice: A sense of who we are.* Portsmouth, NH: Heinemann.

Reed, H. B. and Loughran, E. L. (eds.). (1984). *Beyond schools: Education for economic, social and personal development.* Amherst, MA: Citizen Involvement Training Program.

Reed, S. (ed.). (Winter 1986). 56 Partnership ideas for business. *Instructor*, p. 50.

Rogers, V. R. (1985). Qualitative and aesthetic views of curriculum and curriculum making. *Current thought on curriculum, 1985 ASCD Yearbook* (pp. 103–

17). Alexandria, VA: Association for Supervision and Curriculum Development.

Rossi, P. H. and Freeman, H. E. (1982). *Evaluation: A systematic approach* (2d ed.). Beverly Hills, CA: Sage Publications.

Sarason, S. B. (1971). *The culture of the school and the problem of change* (1st ed.). Boston: Allyn and Bacon.

———. (1972). *The creation of settings and the future societies.* San Francisco: Jossey-Bass.

———. (1982). *The culture of the school and the problem of change* (2d ed.). Boston: Allyn and Bacon.

———. (1983). *Schooling in America: Scapegoat and salvation.* New York: Free Press.

———. (1984). Two cultures meet: The Queens College/Louis Armstrong Middle School collaboration. In S. Trubowitz, J. Duncan, W. Fibkins, P. Longo, and S. Sarason, *When a college works with a public school* (pp. 17–27). Boston: Institute for Responsive Education.

Savitt, S. D. (1986). The planning, implementation, and evaluation of modules designed to provide school personnel with training in the area of parent/school interaction. Ed.D. diss., University of Massachusetts at Amherst.

School Administrator, 42 (February 1985), 16–19 and (March 1985), 22–25.

Schutz, A. (1962). *Collected papers I: The problem of social reality.* The Hague, Netherlands: Martinus Nijhoff.

———. (1964). *Collected papers II: Studies in social theory.* The Hague, Netherlands: Martinus Nijhoff.

———. (1967). *The phenomenology of the social world.* Evanston, IL: Northwestern University Press.

Schutz, A., and Luckmann, T. (1973). *The structures of the life-world.* Evanston, IL: Northwestern University Press.

Scott, H. (1980). *The Black school superintendent: Messiah or scapegoat?* Washington, DC: Howard University Press.

Sieber, S. D. (1981). Knowledge utilization in public education: Incentives and disincentives. In R. Lehming and M. Kane (eds.), *Improving schools: Using what we know* (pp. 115–67). Beverly Hills, CA: Sage Publications.

Silberman, C. E. (1970). *Crisis in the classroom.* New York: Random House.

Sizer, T. R. (1984). *Horace's compromise: The dilemma of the American high school.* Boston: Houghton Mifflin.

Stec, P. J. (1978). Staff development: Approaches in theory and practice. Ed.D. diss., University of Massachusetts at Amherst.

Sweeney, T. A. (1978). The Education for Community Service program: An interpretation of a university and community collaborative teacher education model. Ed.D. diss., University of Massachusetts at Amherst.

Task Force on Education for Economic Growth. (1983). *Action for excellence: A comprehensive plan to improve our nation's schools.* Denver, CO: Education Commission of the States.

Timpane, M. (February 1984). Business has rediscovered the public schools. *Phi Delta Kappan,* pp. 389–92.

Torbert, W. (1976). *Creating a community of inquiry: Conflict, collaboration, transformation.* New York: Wiley.

Trubowitz, S., Duncan, J., Fibkins, W., Longo, P., and Sarason, S. (1984). *When a college works with a public school: A case study of school-college collaboration.* Boston: Institute for Responsive Education.

Tyack, D. (1974). *The one best system: A history of American urban education.* Cambridge, MA: Harvard University Press.

Tyack, D., and Hansot, E. (1982). *Managers of virtue: Public school leadership in America, 1820–1980.* New York: Basic Books.

Tye, K., and Tye, B. (January 1984). Teacher isolation and school reform. *Phi Delta Kappan,* pp. 319–22.

United States Department of Education. (1984). *Partnerships in education.* Washington, DC: U.S. Government Printing Office.

Waller, W. (1932). *The sociology of teaching.* New York: Wiley.

Weatherley, R. (1979). *Reforming special education: Policy implementation from state level to street level.* Cambridge: MIT Press.

Weatherley, R. and Lipsky, M. (1977) Street level bureaucrats and institutional innovation: Implementing special education in Massachusetts. Joint Center for Urban Studies of MIT and Harvard University, Working Paper 44. Unpublished manuscript.

Weick, K. (1976). Educational organizations as loosely coupled systems. *Administrative Science Quarterly, 21*(1), 1–19.

———. (1979). *The social psychology of organizing* (2d ed.). Reading, MA: Addison-Wesley.

———. (June 1982). Administering education in loosely coupled schools. *Phi Delta Kappan,* pp. 673–76.

Wilson, B. L. and Corbett, H. D. (1983). Organization and change: The effects of school linkages on the quantity of implementation. *Educational Administration Quarterly, 19*(4), 85–104.

Winsser, J. (1982). The Education for Community Service program: A description and evaluation of the first five years, 1973–1978. Ed.D. diss., University of Massachusetts at Amherst.

Wise, R. I. (1981). Schools, businesses, and educational needs: From cooperation to collaboration. *Education and Urban Society, 14*(1), 67–82.

Withorn, A. (1982). *The circle game: Services for the poor in Massachusetts, 1966–1978.* Amherst: University of Massachusetts Press.

Woodside, W. S. (July 13, 1986). William S. Woodside on the corporate role. *New York Times,* p. E-8.

Yin, R. K. (1984). *Case study research.* Beverly Hills, CA: Sage Publications.

Zimbardo, P. G., Banks, C. W., Haney, C., and Jaffe, D. (April 8, 1973). A Pirandellian prison. *New York Times Magazine,* pp. 38–53, 56–60.

Index

About the Authors

BYRD L. JONES is Professor of Education at the University of Massachusetts. He is the author of numerous articles, published in such journals as *Journal of Research and Development in Education, Planning & Changing, Change,* and *Urban Education in the 80s.*

ROBERT W. MALOY is Manager of Continuing Education Programs for the School of Education and Adjunct Associate Professor of Education at the University of Massachusetts. He has contributed articles to such diverse publications as *Sociology in Action, Workplace Democracy, Journal of Continuing Higher Education,* and *Continuum.*